Floral knits

Floral knits

25 Contemporary Flower-Inspired Designs

Martin Storey

Photographs by Steven Wooster

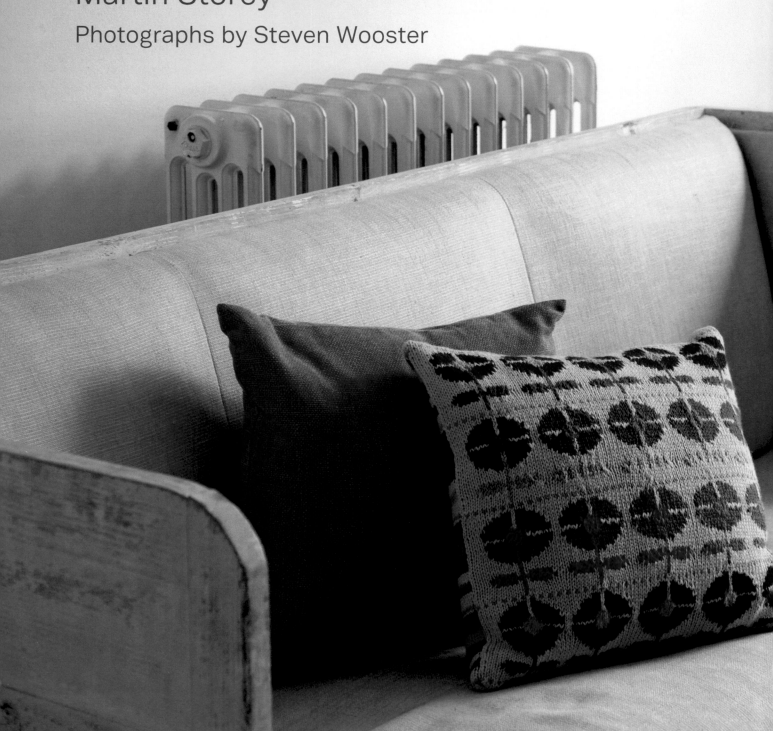

St. Martin's Griffin
New York

Floral Knits

Copyright © 2014 by Berry & Bridges Ltd.

All rights reserved.
Printed in China.
For information, address St. Martin's Press,
175 Fifth Avenue, New York, N.Y. 10010.

www.stmartins.com

Designer Anne Wilson
Editor Katie Hardwicke
Styling Susan Berry
Model Harriet Taylor
Charts Therese Chynoweth
Pattern writing and knitting Penny Hill
Pattern checker Marilyn Wilson

Library of Congress Cataloging-in-Publication Data
Available Upon Request

ISBN 978-1-250-04983-4

St. Martin's Griffin books may be purchased for
educational, business, or promotional use. For
information on bulk purchases, please contact
Macmillan Corporate and Premium Sales
Department at 1-800-221-7945 extension 5442
or write specialmarkets@macmillan.com

First U.S. Edition: May 2014

10 9 8 7 6 5 4 3 2 1

Contents

Introduction

In many ways I could be described as a typical urbanite, but some years ago I moved, with my partner Mark, to the north Devon coast from London. The very great pleasure I experience seeing the seasons change in a singularly beautiful part of Britain, always reminds me of the many and varied joys that nature has to offer. We are lucky here in Ilfracombe to have a great range of scenery: a rugged coastline, wonderful sea views from the windows of our house, and the wild moorland of Exmoor a stone's throw inland, all with a relatively gentle climate. Even more to the point, Mark spends a lot of his time painting the landscape around us, so I would find it hard to ignore nature, even if I wanted to do so!

The opportunity to create a collection of knit designs with a natural, flowery theme gave me a wonderful chance to try something a bit different that reflected my love of nature and color. Like a child with a paintbox, I could try out lots of singing colors in an attempt to capture the vibrancy and variety of forms we see in the flowers around us—from soft, delicate, almost translucent petals to tiny buds not yet unfurled—and to use their colors, shapes, and forms to add a new dimension to my knit designs. They vary from delicate flower appliqués to graphic flower patterns created in colorwork, and from richly textured monochrome flowers to strong simple flower images; they add a touch of difference and distinction to a range of simple garments, accessories, and things for home decoration.

I have gained something of a reputation (if I may say so?) for creating highly textured knits in subtle combinations of color, pattern, and stitch. This collection, however, is something of a departure in that I have used color with greater abandon than is my custom. And I just love the result. In fact, creating the designs, seeing the swatches being knitted up, playing with the embroidery, and tweaking the details with Penny Hill, my masterly knitting technician, plus helping to style the photography for this book, turned out to be a greater delight than I could have hoped for.

Most knitwear designers are under pressure to produce designs against the clock with yarns that are still going through the teething problems inherent in any new product, so imagine the joy of being able to work with yarns I know and love alongside a team of people—photographer, stylist, graphic designer, knitting technician, and editor—whom I respect and with whom I now function as a close-knit team (sorry about the pun!).

This book, in fact, was made all the more fun for me because my niece, Harriet, agreed to model my designs. Although an architecture student rather than a professional model, she impressed us all with her poise, sunny temperament, and her air of being 'à son aise dans sa peau': in other words, very relaxed. (I cannot claim that this latter trait is inherited from her uncle!)

I hope you get the same pleasure in looking at and knitting the designs as we all did in translating them onto the finished pages of this book for you.

Happy knitting!

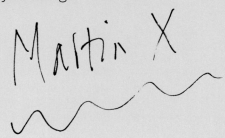

The projects

Posy cardigan

Posy cardigan

Pollen shrug

Pollen wrap

Gardener pillow

Gardener pillow

Floral knits

Marigold runner
and coasters

Flora pillow

Trellis slipover

Trellis slipover

Floral knits

Trellis shrug

Tulip beret

Tulip fingerless gloves

Blossom sweater

Blossom socks

Blossom fingerless gloves

Blossom fingerless gloves

Bloom bag and brooch

Herbaceous pillow

Herbaceous throw

Fleur cardigan

Fleur cardigan

Floral knits

Bouquet bag

Gardenia bolero

Petal pillow

Petal garland

Floral knits

Poppy brooch

Dahlia bag

The patterns

Posy cardigan

This neat, cropped, short-sleeved cardigan has a beautifully placed, show-stopping self-colored design of intricate roses and rose buds that scroll up the front of the cardigan. An heirloom-worthy design to knit for more advanced knitters.

Finished size

To fit bust

32	34	36	38	40	42	44	in
82	86	92	97	102	107	112	cm

ACTUAL MEASUREMENTS

Bust

32½	35½	37½	39½	41¾	44	46½	in
83	90	95	100	106	112	118	cm

Length to shoulder

16¼	16½	17	17¾	18	19	19¼	in
41	42	43	45	46	48	49	cm

Sleeve length

2in/5cm

Yarn

5(5:6:6:7:7:7) x 1¾oz/197yd balls of Rowan *Wool Cotton 4ply* in Leaf 491

Needles

Pair each of size 2 (2.75mm) and size 3 (3.25mm) knitting needles
Cable needle

Extras

8 buttons

Gauge

28 sts and 36 rows to 4in/10cm square measured over St st using size 3 (3.25mm) needles, *or size to obtain correct gauge.*

Abbreviations

C2B = cable 2 back, slip next st onto cable needle and leave at back of work, k1, then k1 from cable needle.
C2F = cable 2 front, slip next st onto cable needle and leave at front of work, k1, then k1 from cable needle.
Cr2R = cross 2 right, slip next st onto cable needle and

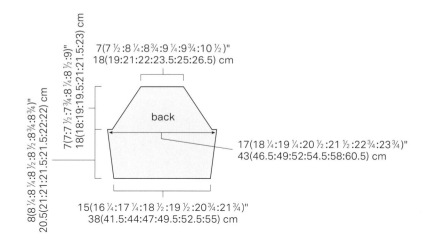

7(7 ½:8 ¼:8 ¾:9 ¼:9 ¾:10 ½)"
18(19:21:22:23.5:25:26.5) cm

7(7:7 ½:7 ¾:8 ¼:8 ½:9)"
18(18:19:19.5:21:21.5:23) cm

back

17(18 ¼:19 ¼:20 ½:21 ½:22 ¾:23 ¾)"
43(46.5:49:52:54.5:58:60.5) cm

8(8 ¼:8 ¼:8 ½:8 ½:8 ¾:8 ¾)"
20.5(21:21:21.5:21.5:22:22) cm

15(16 ¼:17 ¼:18 ½:19 ½:20 ¾:21 ¾)"
38(41.5:44:47:49.5:52.5:55) cm

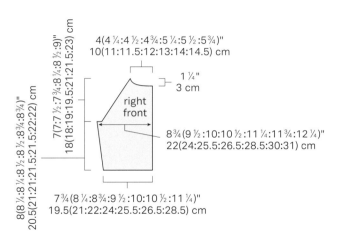

4(4 ¼:4 ½:4 ¾:5 ¼:5 ½:5 ¾)"
10(11:11.5:12:13:14:14.5) cm

1 ¼"
3 cm

right
front

7(7:7 ½:7 ¾:8 ¼:8 ½:9)"
18(18:19:19.5:21:21.5:23) cm

8(8 ¼:8 ¼:8 ½:8 ½:8 ¾:8 ¾)"
20.5(21:21:21.5:21.5:22:22) cm

8 ¾(9 ½:10:10 ½:11 ¼:11 ¾:12 ¼)"
22(24:25.5:26.5:28.5:30:31) cm

7 ¾(8 ¼:8 ¾:9 ½:10:10 ½:11 ¼)"
19.5(21:22:24:25.5:26.5:28.5) cm

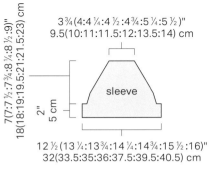

3 ¾(4:4 ¼:4 ½:4 ¾:5 ¼:5 ½)"
9.5(10:11:11.5:12:13.5:14) cm

7(7:7 ½:7 ¾:8 ¼:8 ½:9)"
18(18:19:19.5:21:21.5:23) cm

sleeve

2"
5 cm

12 ½(13 ¼:13 ¾:14 ¼:14 ¾:15 ½:16)"
32(33.5:35:36:37.5:39.5:40.5) cm

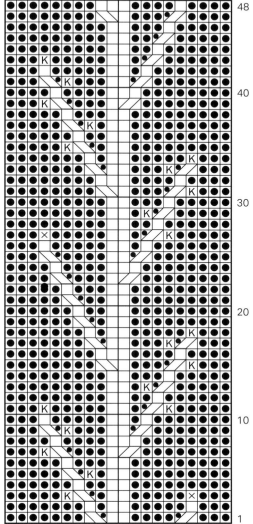

KEY

	K on RS, P on WS
	P on RS, K on WS
	Cr2R
	Cr2L
	C2B
	C2F
K	MK
X	Place rose, then purl this st

leave at back of work, k1, then p1 from cable needle.
Cr2L = cross 2 left, slip next st onto cable needle and leave at front of work, p1, then k1 from cable needle.
MK = make knot, [k1, p1, k1, p1, k1] all into next st, turn and p5, turn, and pass 2nd, 3rd, 4th, and 5th sts over 1st st and off the needle, then k1 tbl into this st to complete knot.
See also page 134.

Note

When working from Chart, odd numbered rows are knit rows and read from right to left. Even numbered rows are purl rows and read from left to right.

Back

Using size 2 (2.75mm) needles, cast on 105(113:121:129:137:145:153) sts.
Rib row 1 (RS) P1, [k1, p1] to end.
Rib row 2 K1, [p1, k1] to end.
These 2 rows form the rib.
Work a further 26 rows.
Change to size 3 (3.25mm) needles.
Beg with a knit row, work in St st.
Work 2 rows.
Inc row K3, M1, knit to last 3 sts, M1, k3.
Work 5 rows.
Rep the last 6 rows 5 times more and the inc row again. *119(127:135:143:151:159:167) sts*
Work 5(7:7:9:9:11:11) rows.

Shape armholes
Bind off 5(6:6:7:7:8:8) sts at beg of next 2 rows.
109(115:123:129:137:143:151) sts
Next row K1, skp, knit to last 3 sts, k2tog, k1.
Next row Purl to end.
Rep the last 2 rows 29(30:32:33:35:36:38) times more.
49(53:57:61:65:69:73) sts
Leave these sts on a spare needle.

Sleeves

Using size 2 (2.75mm) needles, cast on 88(92:96:100:104:108:112) sts.
Rib row (RS) [K1, p1] to end.
Work a further 11 rows.
Change to size 3 (3.25mm) needles.
Beg with a knit row, work in St st.
Work 8 rows.

Shape raglans
Bind off 5(6:6:7:7:8:8) sts at beg of next 2 rows.
78(80:84:86:90:92:96) sts
Next row K1, skp, knit to last 3 sts, k2tog, k1.
Next row Purl to end.
Next row Knit to end.
Next row Purl to end.
Rep the last 4 rows 3(4:5:6:7:8:9) times more.
70(70:72:72:74:74:76) sts
Next row K1, skp, knit to last 3 sts, k2tog, k1.
Next row Purl to end.
Rep the last 2 rows 21(20:20:19:19:18:18) times more.
26(28:30:32:34:36:38) sts
Leave these sts on a spare needle.

Left front

Using size 2 (2.75mm) needles, cast on 58(62:66:70:74:78:82) sts.
Rib row 1 (RS) [K1, p1] to last 2 sts, k2.
Rib row 2 [K1, p1] to end.
These 2 rows form the rib.
Work a further 25 rows.
Next row Rib 11, leave these sts on a holder, cast on one st, rib to end. *48(52:56:60:64:68:72) sts*
Change to size 3 (3.25mm) needles.
Row 1 K26(30:34:38:42:46:50), work across row 25 of Chart, k2.
Row 2 P2, work across row 26 of Chart, p26(30:34:38:42:46:50).
These 2 rows set the chart.
Inc row K3, M1, patt to end.
Work 5 rows.

Rep the last 6 rows 5 times more and the inc row again. *55(59:63:67:71:75:79) sts*
Work 5(7:7:9:9:11:11) rows.

Shape armhole
Next row Bind off 5(6:6:7:7:8:8) sts, patt to end.
50(53:57:60:64:67:71) sts
Next row Patt to end.
Next row K1, skp, patt to end.
Next row Patt to end.
Rep the last 2 rows 23(24:26:27:29:30:32) times more.
26(28:30:32:34:36:38) sts

Shape front neck
Next row K1, skp, patt13(14:15:16:17:18:19), turn and work on these 15(16:17:18:19:20:21) sts for first side of neck shaping, leave rem sts on a spare needle.
Next row Bind off 2(3:4:5:6:7:8) sts, patt to end. *13 sts*
Next row K1, skp, patt to last 3 sts, k2tog, k1.
Next row Patt to end.
Rep the last 2 rows 4 times more. *3 sts*
Leave these sts on a spare needle.

Buttonband
With RS facing, using size 2 (2.75mm) needles, cast on one st, then rib across 11 sts on left front holder.
12 sts
Cont in rib as set until band fits up left front to neck shaping, ending with a WS row.
Leave these sts on a holder.
Place markers for buttons, the first on the 5th row from cast-on edge, the eigth will come on the 5th row of neckband, with 6 spaced evenly between.

Right front
Using size 2 (2.75mm) needles, cast on 58(62:66:70:74:78:82) sts.
1st row K2, [p1, k1] to end.
2nd row [P1, k1] to end.
Rep the last 2 rows once more.
Buttonhole row Rib 5, yo, p2tog, rib to end.

Work remaining buttonholes to match.

Work a further 22 rows, ending with a first row.

Next row Rib to last 11 sts, leave these sts on a holder, cast on one st. *48(52:56:60:64:68:72) sts*

Change to size 3 (3.25mm) needles.

Row 1 K2, work across row 1 of Chart, k26(30:34:38:42:46:50).

Row 2 P26(30:34:38:42:46:50), work across row 2 of Chart, p2.

These 2 rows set the chart.

Inc row Patt to last 3 sts, M1, patt to end.

Work 5 rows.

Rep the last 6 rows 5 times more and the inc row again. *55(59:63:67:71:75:79) sts*

Work 6(8:8:10:10:12:12) rows.

Shape armhole

Next row Bind off 5(6:6:7:7:8:8) sts, patt to end. *50(53:57:60:64:67:71) sts*

Next row Patt to last 3 sts, k2tog, k1.

Next row Patt to end.

Rep the last 2 rows 23(24:26:27:29:30:32) times more. *26(28:30:32:34:36:38) sts*

Shape front neck

Next row Patt 10(11:12:13:14:15:16), place these sts on a holder, patt to last 3 sts, k2tog, k1. *15(16:17:18:19:20:21) sts*

Next row Patt to end.

Next row Bind off 3(4:5:6:7:8:9) sts, patt to last 3 sts, k2tog, k1. *11 sts*

Next row Patt to end.

Next row K1, skp, patt to last 3 sts, k2tog, k1.

Rep the last 2 rows 3 times more. *3 sts*

Next row Patt to end.

Leave these sts on a spare needle.

Buttonhole band

With wrong side facing, using size 2 (2.75mm) needles, cast on one st, then rib across 11 sts on right front holder. *12 sts*

Working buttonholes to match markers, cont in rib as set until band fits up right front to neck shaping, ending with a wrong side row.

Neckband

With right side facing, using size 2 (2.75mm) needles, rib 10, p2tog, across buttonhole band, k2tog, k8(9:10:11:12:13:14) from right front holder, pick up and k8 sts up right side of front neck, k1, skp from holder, k2tog, k22(24:26:28:30:32:34), skp, across right sleeve, k2tog, k45(49:53:57:61:65:69) across back neck sts, skp, k2tog, k22(24:26:28:30:32:34), skp, across left sleeve, k2tog, k1 from holder, pick up and k8 sts down left side of front neck, k8(9:10:11:12:13:14), skp, from left front holder, p2tog, rib 10, from buttonband. *155(165:175:185:195:205:215) sts*

Work 3 rows in rib as set.

Buttonhole row Rib 5, yo, p2tog, rib to end.

Work a further 5 rows.

Bind off in rib.

Roses (make 6)

Using size 2 (2.75mm) needles, cast on 28 sts.

Row 1 (RS) [K1, p1] to end.

Row 2 As row 1.

Row 3 [K1, purl into front and back of next st] to end. *42 sts*

Row 4 [K2, purl into front and back of next st] to end. *56 sts*

Row 5 [K2, p2] to end.

Row 6 As row 5.

Bind off.

Roll cast-on edge to create Rose shape and secure in place.

Finishing

Join raglan and seams. Sew front bands in place. Join side and sleeve seams. Sew on buttons. Sew one rose to each st marked with an "X," omitting row 3 on right front.

Pollen shrug

This easy shrug with a wide shawl collar and deep ribbed hem, ideal for wearing over a summer dress on a cool evening, is dressed up with the addition of lots of little self-colored flowers attached to the sleeves over their placement bobbles in the pattern.

Finished size

To fit bust

32–34	36–38	40–42	in
82–86	92–97	102–107	cm

ACTUAL MEASUREMENTS

Length (cuff to cuff)

33¾	37¾	41¾	in
86	96	106	cm

Length (excluding border)

10¾	12¼	13½	in
27.5	31	34.5	cm

Sleeve length

5½ in/14cm

Yarn

6(7:8) x 1¾oz/197yd balls of Rowan *Wool Cotton 4ply* in Old Rose 448

Needles

Pair each of size 2 (2.75mm) and size 3 (3.25mm) knitting needles
Circular size 3 (3.25mm) needle
Size 6 (4mm) needle

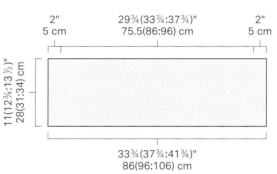

2"
5 cm

29¾(33¾:37¾)"
75.5(86:96) cm

2"
5 cm

11(12¾:13½)"
28(31:34) cm

33¾(37¾:41¾)"
86(96:106) cm

Gauge

28 sts and 36 rows to 4in/10cm measured over St st using size 3 (3.25mm) needles, *or size to obtain correct gauge.*

Abbreviations

MB = make bobble, [k1, yf, k1, yf, k1] all into next st, turn, p5, turn, k5, turn, p2tog, p1, p2tog, turn, sk2p. See also page 134.

Shrug

Using size 2 (2.75mm) needles, cast on 77(87:97) sts.
Knit 3 rows.
Change to size 3 (3.25mm) needles.
Row 1 Knit to end.
Row 2 Purl to end.
Rows 3 to 6 Rep rows 1 and 2 twice.
Row 7 K3, [MB, k9] to last 4 sts, MB, k3.
Row 8 As row 2.
Rows 9 to 20 Rep rows 1 and 2 six times.
Row 21 K8, [MB, k9] to last 9 sts, MB, k8.
Row 22 As row 2.
Rows 23 to 28 Rep rows 1 and 2 three times.
Rep rows 1 to 22 again.
Mark each end of last row with a colored thread.
Cont in St st until piece measures 28¼(32¼:36¼)in/ 72(82:92)cm from cast-on edge, ending with a purl row.
Mark each end of last row with a colored thread
Row 1 K8, [MB, k9] to last 9 sts, MB, k8.
Row 2 Purl to end.
Rows 3 to 14 Rep rows 1 and 2 six times.
Row 15 K3, [MB, k9] to last 4 sts, MB, k3.
Row 16 As row 2.
Rows 17 to 28 Rep rows 1 and 2 six times.
Rep rows 1 to 22 again.
Knit 3 rows.
Bind off.

Flowers (make 60[68:76])

Using size 2 (2.75mm) needles, cast on 57 sts.
Row 1 Purl to end.
Row 2 K2, [k1, slip this st back onto left-hand needle, lift next 8 sts on left-hand needle over this st and off left-hand needle, y2rn, knit st on left-hand needle again, k2] to end. *27 sts*
Row 3 K1, [p2tog, then k1, k1 tbl, k1, k1 tbl all into y2rn, p1] to last st, k1. *32 sts*
Row 4 [K2tog] 16 times.
Break yarn, thread through rem sts, slip center over bobble, fasten off securely. Sew row ends of flower together.

Border

Using circular size 3 (3.25mm) needle, with right side facing, pick up and k156(186:216) sts between colored threads on one side, with wrong sides together fold shrug in half, pick up and k156(186:216) sts between colored threads on second side. *312(372:432) sts*
Cont in rounds:
Round 1 [K1, p2] to end of round.
Round 2 [K1, M1, p2] to end of round. *416(496:576) sts*
Round 3 [K2, p2] to end of round.
Rep the last round for 6(6¼:6¾)in/15(16:17)cm.
Using a size 6 (4mm) needle, bind off in rib.

Finishing

Join sleeve seams from colored threads to cast-on/ bound-off edge.

Pollen wrap

The same flowers used in the Pollen shrug are translated into a multicolored decoration on a generous wrap, knitted in Rowan *Wool Cotton 4ply*. The flowers are added to the bobbles that create their centers. You can add as many rows of flowers as you have the inclination to knit the bobbles for them!

Finished size
17¾in/45cm wide by 67in/ 170cm long

Yarn
Rowan *Wool Cotton 4ply*
7 x 1¾oz/197yd balls in Leaf 491
Flowers
Small amount each in Flower 485, Rich 493, Butter 488, Satsuma 489, Jacaranda 502, Hedge 494, Antique 480, and Aqua 487

Needles
Pair each of size 3 (3.25mm) and size 2 (2.75mm) knitting needles

Gauge
28 sts and 36 rows to 4in/10cm measured over St st using size 3 (3.25mm) needles, *or size to obtain correct gauge.*

Abbreviations
MB = make bobble, [k1, yf, k1, yf, k1] all into next st, turn, p5, turn, k5, turn, p2tog, p1, p2tog, turn, sk2p. See also page 134.

Wrap (make 2 pieces)
Using size 3 (3.25mm) needles, cast on 127 sts.
Knit 3 rows.
Row 1 Knit to end,
Row 2 K3, purl to last 3 sts, k3.
Rows 3 to 6 Rep rows 1 and 2 twice.
Row 7 K3, [MB, k9] to last 4 sts, MB, k3.
Row 8 As row 2.
Rows 9 to 20 Rep rows 1 and 2 six times.
Row 21 K8, [MB, k9] to last 9 sts, MB, k8.
Row 22 As row 2.
Rows 23 to 28 Rep rows 1 and 2 three times.

Rep rows 1 to 28 once more, then rows 1 to 22 again.

Cont in St st with garter-st edge until piece measures 33 ½ in/85cm from cast-on edge, ending with a wrong side row.

Leave sts on a spare needle.

Finishing

With needles pointing in the same direction and right sides together, bind off the sts of both pieces together.

Flowers (make 19 in each of 6 colors and 18 in each of 2 colors, total 150)

Using size 2 (2.75mm) needles, cast on 57 sts.

Row 1 Purl to end.

Row 2 K2, [k1, slip this st back onto left-hand needle, lift next 8 sts on left-hand needle over this st and off left-hand needle, y2rn, knit st on left-hand needle again, k2] to end. *27 sts*

Row 3 K1, [p2tog, then k1, k1 tbl, k1, k1 tbl all into y2rn, p1] to last st, k1. *32 sts*

Row 4 [K2tog] 16 times.

Break yarn, thread through rem sts, slip center over bobble, fasten off securely. Sew row ends of flower together.

Gardener pillow

With its Art Nouveau stylized flower design, this great pillow works in both contemporary and traditional settings. Knitted with a black background it gains sophistication, but you could knit one with a white ground for a ligher, more summery feel.

Finished size
To fit 16in/40cm square pillow form

Yarns
Rowan *Wool Cotton*
3 x 1¾oz/123yd balls in Inky 908 (MC)
2 x 1¾oz/123yd balls in Elf 946 (A)
1 x 1¾oz/123yd ball each in Rich 911 (B) and Cypress 968 (C)

Needles
Pair of size 5 (3.75mm) knitting needles

Extras
12in/30cm zipper
16in/40cm square pillow form

Gauge
24 sts and 30 rows to 4in/10cm measured over St st using size 5 (3.75mm) needles, *or size to obtain correct gauge*. 26 sts and 30 rows to 4in/10cm measured over patt using size 5 (3.75mm) needles, *or size to obtain correct gauge*.

Abbreviations
See page 134.

Note
When working from Chart, odd numbered rows are knit rows and read from right to left. Even numbered rows are purl rows and read from left to right.

Front
Using size 5 (3.75mm) needles and MC, cast on 105 sts.
Beg with a knit row, work in St st.
Work 6 rows.
Work in patt from Chart.

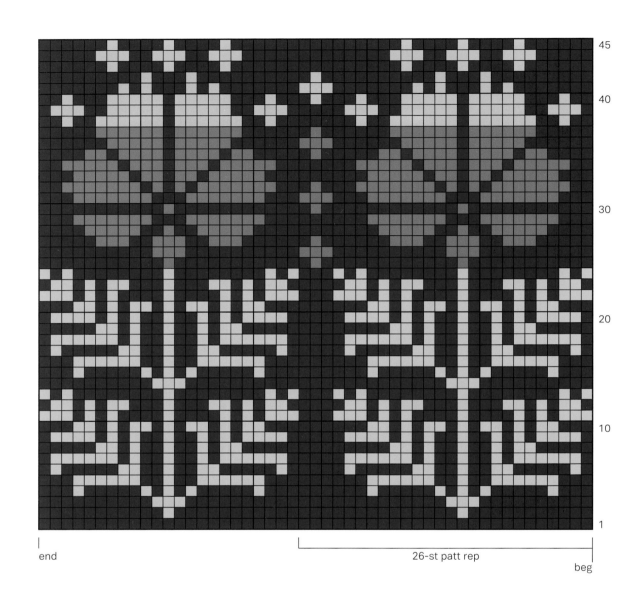

Floral knits

Row 1 K2MC, [work 26 sts of 1st row of Chart] 3 times, work last 23 sts of Chart, k2MC

Row 2 P2MC, work first 23 sts of Chart, [work 26 sts of 2nd row of Chart] 3 times, p2MC.

These 2 rows set the position for the Chart.

Cont in patt to end of row 45.

Work 7 rows in MC.

Work rows 1 to 45 from Chart.

Work 6 rows in MC.

Bind off.

Back

Using size 5 (3.75mm) needles and MC, cast on 93 sts.

Beg with a knit row, work in St st and stripe sequence as foll:

6 rows MC, ** [2 rows A, 2 rows MC] 6 times, 4 rows B, 1 row MC, 3 rows B, 1 row MC, 4 rows B, 5 rows C, 3 rows A **, 7 rows MC.

Rep from ** to ** once more.

Work 6 rows MC.

Using MC, bind off.

Finishing

Leaving 12in/30cm opening for zipper, join bottom seam. With right sides together, sew remaining seams. Turn to right side. Insert pillow form.

Marigold runner

This project is ideal if you want to knit on the go, as you make up the individual squares (which serve as the coasters, too) and then join them together for the runner or, indeed, for a couple of pillows.

Finished size
12in/30cm x 59in/150cm

Yarns
Rowan *Wool Cotton*
2 x 1¾oz/123yd balls each in Rich 911, Cypress 968, Tender 951, and Elf 946
1 x 1¾oz/123yd ball each in Café 985, Flower 943, and Bilberry 969
These quantities will also make the matching coasters

Needles
Pair of size 3 (3.25mm) knitting needles

Gauge
25 sts and 32 rows to 4in/10cm measured over St st using size 3 (3.25mm) needles, *or size to obtain correct gauge.*

Abbreviations
See page 134.

Note
When working the motif use the Fairisle method, strand the yarn not in use across the wrong side of work, weaving them under and over the working yarn every 3 or 4 sts.
When working from Chart, odd numbered rows are knit rows and read from right to left. Even numbered rows are purl rows and read from left to right.

Square 1 (make 5)
(use Elf 946 for flower)
Using size 3 (3.25mm) needles and Rich 911, leaving a 8in/20cm end, cast on 37 sts.
Rows 1 to 4 K1, [p1, k1] to end.
Row 5 K1, p1, knit to last 2 sts, p1, k1.

Row 6 K1, p1, k1, purl to last 3 sts, k1, p1, k1.

These 2 rows form the St st with seed st borders.

Working from row 7 on Chart, complete the square.

Leaving a 8in/20cm end, bind off in seed st.

Square 2 (make 5)

(use Café 985 for flower)

Using size 3 (3.25mm) needles and Cypress 968, leaving a 8in/20cm end, cast on 37 sts.

Work as given for Square 1.

Square 3 (make 5)

(use Flower 943 for flower)

Using size 3 (3.25mm) needles and Tender 951, leaving a 8in/20cm end, cast on 37 sts.

Work as given for Square 1.

Square 4 (make 5)

(use Bilberry 969 for flower)

Using size 3 (3.25mm) needles and Elf 946, leaving a 8in/20cm end, cast on 37 sts.

Work as given for Square 1.

Finishing

Join squares together to form a runner 2 squares wide by 10 squares long.

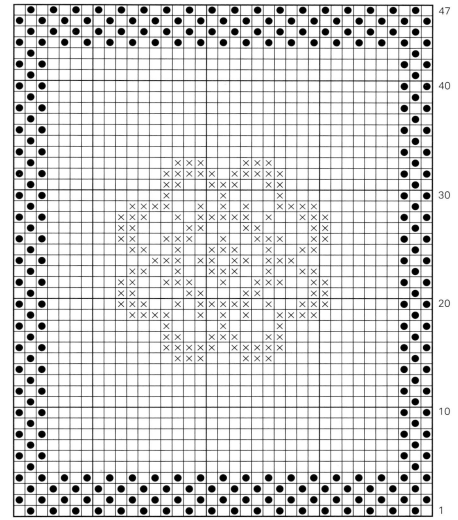

KEY

Background color

☐ K on RS, P on WS

◉ P on RS, K on WS

Flower color

☒ K on RS, P on WS

Marigold coasters

This matching set of four coasters complements the table runner perfectly. You can, of course, make as many coasters as you like in different color combinations to match whatever is left over in your yarn stash.

Finished size
Size 6in / 15cm square

Yarns
Rowan *Wool Cotton*
1 x 1¾oz/123yd ball each in Café 985, Flower 943, and Bilberry 969
Small amount each in Café 985, Flower 943, and Bilberry 969

Needles
Pair of size 3 (3.25mm) knitting needles

Gauge
25 sts and 32 rows to 4in/10cm measured over St st using size 3 (3.25mm) needles, *or size to obtain correct gauge.*

Abbreviations
See page 134.

Note
When working the motif use the Fairisle method, strand the yarn not in use across the wrong side of work, weaving them under and over the working yarn every 3 or 4 sts.
When working from Chart, odd numbered rows are knit rows and read from right to left. Even numbered rows are purl rows and read from left to right.

Square 1
(use Elf 946 for flower)
Using size 3 (3.25mm) needles and Rich 911, leaving a 8in/20cm end, cast on 37 sts.
Rows 1 to 4 K1, [p1, k1] to end.
Row 5 K1, p1, knit to last 2 sts, p1, k1.
Row 6 K1, p1, k1, purl to last 3 sts, k1, p1, k1.

These 2 rows form the St st with seed st borders.

Working from row 7 on Chart, complete the square.

Leaving a 8in/20cm end, bind off in seed st.

Square 2

(use Café 985 for flower)

Using size 3 (3.25mm) needles and Cypress 968, leaving a 8in/20cm end, cast on 37 sts.

Work as given for Square 1.

Square 3

(use Flower 943 for flower)

Using size 3 (3.25mm) needles and Tender 951, leaving a 8in/20cm end, cast on 37 sts.

Work as given for Square 1.

Square 4

(use Bilberry 969 for flower)

Using size 3 (3.25mm) needles and Elf 946, leaving a 8in/20cm end, cast on 37 sts.

Work as given for Square 1.

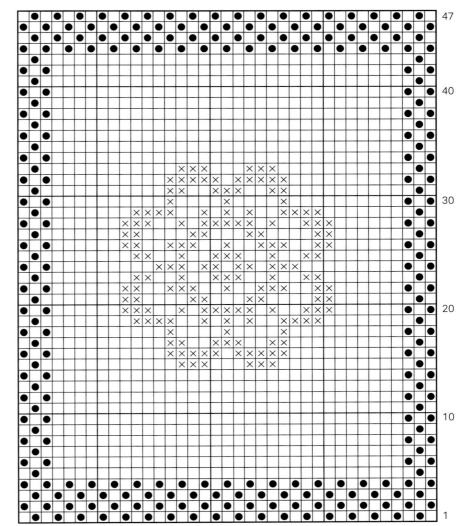

KEY

Background color

☐ K on RS, P on WS

⦿ P on RS, K on WS

Flower color

☒ K on RS, P on WS

Flora pillow

A similar stylized flower design to the Gardener pillow on page 69, this elegant design would work with it as a pair if knitted in similar colors. It makes a great addition to any plain sofa or chair.

Finished size
To fit 16in/40cm square pillow forn

Yarns
Rowan *Wool Cotton*
2 x 1¾oz/123yd balls in Celadon 979 (MC)
1 x 1¾oz/123yd ball each in Cypress 968 (A), Deepest Olive 907 (B), French Navy 909 (C), Pier 983 (D), Rich 911 (E), Bilberry 969 (F), Flower 943 (G), Elf 946 (H), and Ship Shape 955 (I)

Needles
Pair of size 5 (3.75mm) knitting needles

Extras
12in/30cm zipper
16in/40cm square pillow form

Gauge
24 sts and 30 rows to 4in/10cm measured over St st using size 5 (3.75mm) needles, *or size to obtain correct gauge.*

Abbreviations
See page 134.

Note
When working from Chart, odd numbered rows are knit rows and read from right to left. Even numbered rows are purl rows and read from left to right.

Front
Using size 5 (3.75mm) needles and MC, cast on 93 sts.
Beg with a knit row, work in St st.
Work 2 rows.
Work in patt from Chart.

Row 1 Using MC, knit to end.

Row 2 P1MC, [1A, 1MC] to end..

Row 3 Using MC, knit to end.

Row 4 [P3MC, work 15 sts of 4th row of Chart] 5 times, p3MC.

Row 5 K3MC, [work 15 sts of 5th row of Chart, k3MC] 5 times.

These 2 rows set the position for the Chart.

Cont in patt to end of row 81, noting rows 29 and 56 will read:

Row 29 K1MC, [1A, 1MC] to end.

Row 56 P1MC, [1A, 1MC] to end.

Now work rows 1 to 30 again.

Work 2 rows in MC.

Bind off.

Back

Using size 5 (3.75mm) needles and MC, cast on 93 sts.

Beg with a knit row, work in St st and stripe sequence as foll:

3 rows MC, 1 row A, 4 rows MC, 3 rows B, 3 rows MC, 5 rows C, 5 rows D, 5 rows C, 1 row MC, 1 row A, 4 rows MC, 3 rows E, 3 rows MC, 5 rows F, 5 rows G, 5 rows F, 1 row MC, 1 row A, 4 rows MC, 3 rows H, 3 rows MC, 5 rows B, 5 rows I, 5 rows B, 1 row MC, 1 row A, 4 rows MC, 3 rows B, 3 rows MC, 5 rows C, 5 rows D, 5 rows C, 1 row MC, 1 row A, 3 rows MC.

Using MC, bind off.

Finishing

Leaving 12in/30cm opening for zipper, join bottom seam. With right sides together, sew remaining seams. Turn to right side. Insert pillow form.

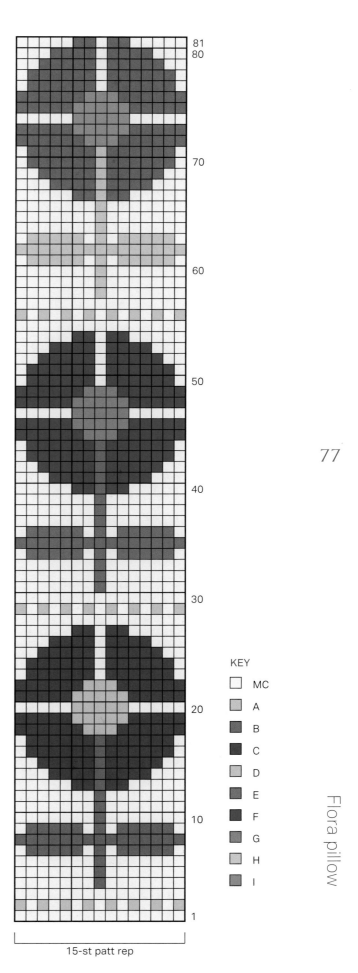

KEY

☐	MC
☐	A
☐	B
☐	C
☐	D
☐	E
☐	F
☐	G
☐	H
☐	I

15-st patt rep

Trellis slipover

This pretty slipover with its trellis design made of bobbles, scattered with different colored simple embroidered flowers in yarn, dresses up a plain skirt or pants and adds a feminine touch.

Finished size

To fit bust

32–34	36–38	40–42	in
82–86	92–97	102–107	cm

ACTUAL MEASUREMENTS

Bust

34 ½	38 ½	42 ½	in
87	98	108	cm

Length to shoulder

20	20 ¾	21 ¾	in
51	53	55	cm

Yarn

6(7:7) x 1 ¾ oz/197yd balls of Rowan *Wool Cotton 4ply* in Antique 480
Small amounts of assorted colors for embroidery

Needles

Pair each of size 2 (2.75mm) and size 3 (3.25mm) knitting needles

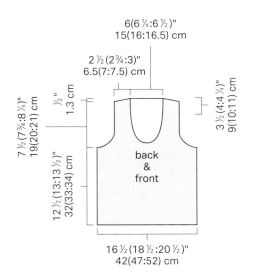

6(6 ¼:6 ½)"
15(16:16.5) cm

2 ½ (2¾:3)"
6.5(7:7.5) cm

½"
1.3 cm

3 ½ (4:4 ¼)"
9(10:11) cm

7 ½ (7¾:8 ¼)"
19(20:21) cm

12 ½ (13:13 ½)"
32(33:34) cm

back & front

16 ½ (18 ½:20 ½)"
42(47:52) cm

Gauge

28 sts and 36 rows to 4in/10cm measured over St st using size 3 (3.25mm) needles, *or size to obtain correct gauge.* 30 sts and 33 rows to 4in/10cm measured over patt using size 3 (3.25mm) needles, *or size to obtain correct gauge.*

Abbreviations

MB = make bobble, [k1, p1, k1] all into next st, turn, p3, turn, k3, turn, p3, turn, sk2p.
See also page 134.

Note

When working from Chart, odd numbered rows are knit rows and read from right to left. Even numbered rows are purl rows and read from left to right.

Slipover

Using size 2 (2.75mm) needles, cast on 131(147:163) sts.

Row 1 P1, [k1, p1] to end.
Row 2 K1, [p1, k1] to end.
These 2 rows form the rib.
Work a further 16 rows.
Change to size 3 (3.25mm) needles.
Row 1 P1, [k1, p1] to end.
Row 2 K1, [p1, k1] to end.

Row 3 P1, [MB, p1, k1, p1] to last 2 sts, MB, p1.
Row 4 As row 2.
Rows 5 and 6 As rows 1 and 2.
Work from Chart.
Row 1 P1, [work row 1 of 16-st rep] 8(9:10) times, work last st of Chart, p1.
Row 2 K1, work first st of Chart, [work row 2 of 16-st rep] 8(9:10) times, k1.
These 2 rows set the patt.
Cont in patt until work measures 12 ½ (13:13 ½)in/ 32(33:34)cm from cast-on edge, ending with a wrong side row.

Shape armholes

Bind off 12(14:16) sts at beg of next 2 rows. *107(119:131) sts*
Next row Skp, patt to last 2 sts, k2tog.
Next row P2tog, patt to last 2 sts, p2tog tbl.
Rep the last 2 rows 1(2:3) time(s) more. *99(107:115) sts ***
Next row Skp, patt to last 2 sts, k2tog.
Next row Patt to end.
Rep the last 2 rows 6(7:8) times more. *85(91:97) sts*
Keeping edge sts in rib, work even until back measures 20(20¾:21¾)in/51(53:55)cm from cast-on edge, ending with a wrong side row.

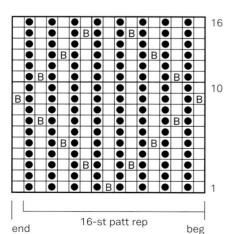

16

10

1

KEY

☐ K on RS, P on WS

⬤ P on RS, K on WS

B MB

end   16-st patt rep   beg

Shape shoulders
Bind off 9(10:11) sts at beg of next 2 rows and 10(11:12) sts at beg of foll 2 rows.
Leave the rem 47(49:51) sts on a spare needle.

Front
Work as given for Back to **.

Shape front neck
Next row Skp, patt 37(40:43), k2tog, turn, and work on these 39(42:45) sts for first side of neck shaping.
Next row Patt to end.
Next row Skp, patt to last 2 sts, k2tog.
Next row Patt to end.
Rep the last 2 rows 5(6:7) times more. *27(28:29) sts*
Keeping armhole edge straight, cont to dec at neck edge on every **4th** row until 19(21:23) sts rem.
Work even until front measures the same as back to shoulder, ending at armhole edge.

Shape shoulder
Next row Bind off 9(10:11) sts, patt to end.
Patt 1 row.
Bind off rem 10(11:12) sts.
With right side facing, place center 17(19:21) sts on a holder, rejoin yarn to rem sts, skp, patt to last 2 sts, k2tog.
Next row Patt to end.
Next row Skp, patt to last 2 sts, k2tog.
Next row Patt to end.
Rep the last 2 rows 5(6:7) times more. *27(28:29) sts*
Keeping armhole edge straight cont to dec at neck edge on every **4th** row until 19(21:23) sts rem.
Work even until front measures the same as back to shoulder, ending at armhole edge.

Shape shoulder
Next row Bind off 9(10:11) sts, patt to end.
Patt 1 row.
Bind off rem 10(11:12) sts.

Neckband
Join right shoulder seam.
With right side facing, using size 2 (2.75mm) needles, pick up and k53(56:59) sts down left side of front neck, rib 17(19:21) sts from front neck holder, pick up and k52(55:58) sts up right side of front neck, rib across 47(49:51) sts from back neck holder. *169(179:189) sts*
Work 7 rows in rib as set.
Bind off in rib.

Armbands
Join left shoulder seam and neckband.
With right side facing, using size 2 (2.75mm) needles, pick up and k136(146:156) sts evenly around armhole edge.
Work 7 rows k1, p1 rib.
Bind off in rib.

Finishing
Work embroidered flowers using five-petalled lazy daisy stitch and a French knot in the center in a contrasting color (see page 133). Place flowers in center of trellis pattern on alternate rows, as shown.
Join side seams.

Trellis slipover

Trellis shrug

This very simple version of the design works well as a cozy cover-up for a summer frock or an evening dress. A great project to practice some textural stitches as well as trying your hand at a bit of simple embroidery!

Finished size

To fit bust

32–34	36–38	40–42	in
82–86	92–97	102–107	cm

ACTUAL MEASUREMENTS

Length (cuff to cuff)

26	30	34	in
66	76	86	cm

Length

11	13	15	in
28	33	39½	cm

Sleeve length

2in/5cm

Yarn

3(4:5) x 1¾oz/197yd balls of Rowan *Wool Cotton 4ply* in Antique 480
Small amounts of assorted colors for embroidery

Needles

Pair each of size 2 (2.75mm) and size 3 (3.25mm) knitting needles

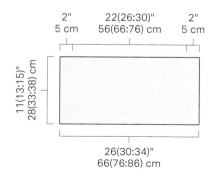

2"
5 cm

22(26:30)"
56(66:76) cm

2"
5 cm

11(13:15)"
28(33:38) cm

26(30:34)"
66(76:86) cm

Gauge

28 sts and 36 rows to 4in/10cm measured over St st using size 3 (3.25mm) needles, *or size to obtain correct gauge.* 30 sts and 33 rows to 4in/10cm measured over patt using size 3 (3.25mm) needles, *or size to obtain correct gauge.*

Abbreviations

MB = make bobble, [k1, p1, k1] all into next st, turn, p3, turn, k3, turn, p3, turn, sk2p.
See also page 134.

Note

When working from Chart, odd numbered rows are knit rows and read from right to left. Even numbered rows are purl rows and read from left to right.

Shrug

Using size 2 (2.75mm) needles, cast on 85(101:117) sts.
Row 1 P2, [k1, p1] to last 3 sts, k1, p2.
Row 2 P1, [k1, p1] to end.
Row 3 P2, [MB, p1, k1, p1] to last 3 sts, MB, p2.
Row 4 As row 2.
Rows 5 and 6 As rows 1 and 2.
Change to size 3 (3.25mm) needles.

Work from Chart.
Row 1 P2, [work row 1 of 16-st rep] 5(6:7) times, work last st of Chart, p2.
Row 2 P1, k1, work first st of Chart, [work row 2 of 16-st rep] 5(6:7) times, k1, p1.
These 2 rows set the patt.
Cont in patt until work measures approx 25½(29½:33½)in/65(75:85)cm from cast-on edge, ending with row 1.
Change to size 2 (2.75mm) needles.
Row 1 P1, [k1, p1] to end.
Row 2 P2, [k1, p1] to last 3 sts, k1, p2.
Row 3 As row 1.
Row 4 P2, [MB, p1, k1, p1] to last 3 sts, MB, p2.
Rows 5 and 6 As rows 1 and 2.
Bind off in rib.

Finishing

Join sleeve seams from cast-on/bound-off edges for approx 2in/5cm.
Work embroidered flowers using five-petaled lazy daisy stitch and a French knot in the center in a contrasting color (see page 133). Place flowers in center of trellis pattern on alternate rows, as shown.

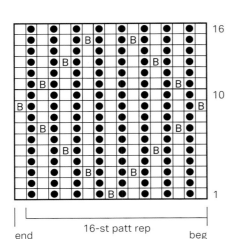

16

10

1

end   16-st patt rep   beg

KEY

☐ K on RS, P on WS

⬤ P on RS, K on WS

B MB

Tulip beret

With a retro look, this generous beret has an eye-catching stylized tulip design around the edge. Knit it and practice your skills with both Fairisle and intarsia colorwork in a small project.

Finished size
To fit an average-sized head

Yarns
Rowan *Wool Cotton*
2 x 1¾oz/123yd balls in Antique 900 (MC)
1 x 1¾oz/123yd ball each in Flower 943 (A), Elf 946 (B), Rich 911 (C), and Deepest Olive 907 (D)

Needles
Pair each of size 3 (3.25mm) and size 5 (3.75mm) knitting needles
Circular size 5 (3.75mm) needle

Gauge
24 sts and 30 rows to 4in/10cm measured over St st using size 5 (3.75mm) needles, *or size to obtain correct gauge.*

Abbreviations
See page 134.

Note
When working from Chart, use the Fairisle method for rows 1 to 5, then use the intarsia method for remainder of Chart.

To make
Using size 3 (3.25mm) needles and MC, cast on 98 sts.
Rib row [K1, p1] to end.
This row forms the rib.
Work a further 10 rows.
Change to size 5 (3.75mm) circular needle.
Work backward and forward in patt.
Inc row P2, [M1, p1, M1, p2] to end. *162 sts*
Beg with a knit row, work in St st.
Work 4 rows.

Place Chart

Row 1 K1MC, [knit across row 1 of 20-st patt rep] 8 times, k1MC.

Row 2 P1MC, [purl across row 2 of 20-st patt rep] 8 times, p1MC.

These 2 rows set the Chart.

Cont in patt to end of Chart.

Cont in MC only.

Work 17 rows.

Shape top

Change to pair of size 5 (3.75mm) needles when sts are reduced sufficiently.

Row 1 K1, [k14, k2tog] 10 times, k1.

Row 2 Purl to end.

Row 3 K1, [k13, k2tog] 10 times, k1.

Row 4 Purl to end.

Row 5 K1, [k12, k2tog] 10 times, k1.

Row 6 Purl to end.

Row 7 K1, [k11, k2tog] 10 times, k1.

Row 8 Purl to end.

Row 9 K1, [k10, k2tog] 10 times, k1.

Row 10 Purl to end.

Row 11 K1, [k9, k2tog] 10 times, k1.

Row 12 Purl to end.

Row 13 K1, [k8, k2tog] 10 times, k1.

Row 14 Purl to end.

Row 15 K1, [k7, k2tog] 10 times, k1.

Row 16 Purl to end.

Row 17 K1, [k6, k2tog] 10 times, k1.

Row 18 Purl to end.

Row 19 K1, [k5, k2tog] 10 times, k1.

Row 20 Purl to end.

Row 21 K1, [k4, k2tog] 10 times, k1.

Row 22 Purl to end.

Row 23 K1, [k3, k2tog] 10 times, k1.

Row 24 Purl to end.

Row 25 K1, [k2, k2tog] 10 times, k1.

Row 26 Purl to end.

Row 27 K1, [k1, k2tog] 10 times, k1.

Row 28 Purl to end.

Row 29 K1, [k2tog] 10 times, k1.

Row 30 Purl to end.

Row 31 K1, [k2tog] 5 times, k1.

Break off yarn, thread through rem 7 sts, and fasten off.

Join seam.

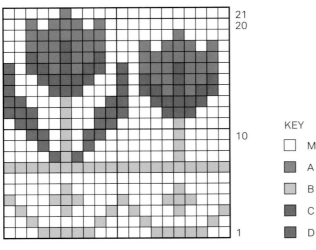

KEY

☐ MC

■ A

■ B

■ C

■ D

Tulip fingerless gloves

These long-length fingerless gloves make a feminine addition to an outfit, bringing a touch of fun. You could knit them with a dark ground and lighter colored flowers for a more dressy look.

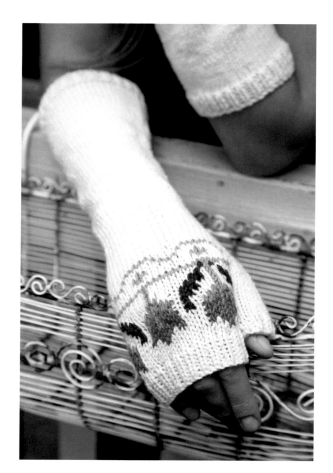

Finished size
To fit small/medium hands
Length 14 ½ in/37cm

Yarns
Rowan *Wool Cotton*
2 x 1¾oz/123yd balls in Antique 900 (MC)
1 x 1¾oz/123yd ball each in Flower 943 (A), Elf 946 (B), Rich 911 (C), and Deepest Olive 907 (D)

Needles
Pair each of size 3 (3.25mm) and size 5 (3.75mm) knitting needles

Gauge
22 sts and 30 rows to 4in/10cm measured over St st using size 5 (3.75mm) needles, *or size to obtain correct gauge.*

Abbreviations
See page 134.

Note
When working from Chart, use the Fairisle method for rows 1 to 5, then use the intarsia method for remainder of Chart.

To make
Using 3.75mm (US 3) needles and MC, cast on 58 sts.
Rib row [K1, p1] to end.
Rep the last row 5 times more, inc one st at center of last row. *59 sts*
Beg with a knit row, work in St st.
Work 14 rows.
Dec row K3, skp, k20, k2tog, k5, skp, k20, k2tog, k3.
Work 13 rows.
Dec row K3, skp, k18, k2tog, k5, skp, k18, k2tog, k3.

Work 13 rows.

Dec row K3, skp, k16, k2tog, k5, skp, k16, k2tog, k3.

Work 13 rows.

Dec row K3, skp, k14, k2tog, k5, skp, k14, k2tog, k3.

Work 13 rows. *43 sts*

Thumb shaping

Row 1 K1, M1, knit to last st, M1, k1.

Row 2 Purl to end.

Row 3 K2, M1, knit to last 2 sts, M1, k2.

Row 4 Purl to end.

Row 5 K3, M1, knit to last 3 sts, M1, k3.

Row 6 Purl to end. *49 sts*

Place chart

Row 1 K4MC, M1, [knit across row 1 of 20-st patt rep] twice, k1MC, M1, k4MC.

Row 2 P6MC, [purl across row 2 of 20-st patt rep] twice, p5MC.

These 2 rows set the Chart.

Cont in this way, inc and work in MC, one st on every right side row until the foll row has been worked.

Row 13 K10MC, M1, [knit across row 13 of 20-st patt rep] twice, k1MC, M1, k10MC. *63 sts*

Row 14 P12, [purl across row 14 of 20-st patt rep] twice, p11.

Row 15 K10, turn, and work on these sts only for thumb.

Beg with a purl row, work 7 rows St st.

Rib row [K1, p1] to end.

Work a further 2 rows.

Bind off in rib.

Next row With right side facing, rejoin yarn to next st, patt to last 12 sts, k12MC.

Next row P10, turn, and work on these sts only for thumb.

Beg with a knit row, work 6 rows St st.

Rib row [K1, p1] to end.

Work a further 2 rows.

Bind off in rib.

Next row With wrong side facing, rejoin yarn to next st, p2, [purl across row 16 of 20-st patt rep] twice, p1. *43 sts*

Work a further 5 rows in patt, ending with a row 21 of Chart.

Using MC, work 2 rows St st, dec one st at center of last row. *42 sts*

Change to size 3 (3.25mm) needles.

Rib row [K1, p1] to end.

Work a further 5 rows.

Bind off in rib.

Finishing

Join side and thumb seams.

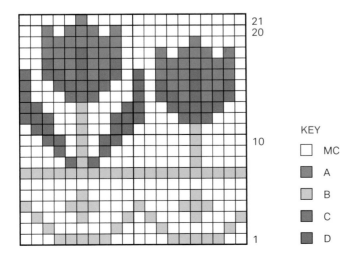

KEY

☐ MC

■ A

■ B

■ C

■ D

Blossom sweater

This lovely retro-style, short-sleeved sweater combines a great cable pattern with some delicate embroidery to make an eye-catching spring sweater. Knit it in white for a more summery look.

Finished size

To fit bust

32–34	36–38	40–42	in
82–86	92–97	102–107	cm

ACTUAL MEASUREMENTS

Bust

34 ¼	39	43 ¾	in
87	99	111	cm

Length to shoulder

22	22 ¾	23 ½	in
56	58	60	cm

Sleeve length

6in/15cm

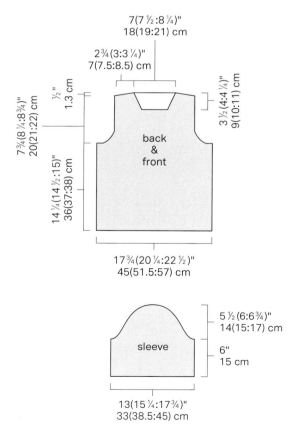

7(7 ½:8 ¼)"
18(19:21) cm

2¾(3:3 ¼)"
7(7.5:8.5) cm

½"
1.3 cm

3 ½ (4:4 ¼)"
9(10:11) cm

7¾(8 ¼:8¾)"
20(21:22) cm

back & front

14 ¼(14 ½:15)"
36(37:38) cm

17¾(20 ¼:22 ½)"
45(51.5:57) cm

5 ½ (6:6¾)"
14(15:17) cm

6"
15 cm

sleeve

13(15 ¼:17¾)"
33(38.5:45) cm

Yarns

Rowan *Wool Cotton 4ply*

7(8:9) x 1¾oz/197yd balls in Flower 485

Small amounts in Leaf 491, Violet 490, and Antique 480 for embroidery

Needles

Pair each of size 2–3 (3mm) and size 3 (3.25mm) knitting needles

Cable needle

Gauge

28 sts and 36 rows to 4in/10cm over St st using size 3 (3.25mm) needles, *or size to obtain correct gauge.*

30 sts and 37 rows to 4in/10cm over patt using size 3 (3.25mm) needles, *or size to obtain correct gauge.*

Abbreviations

C4B = cable 4 back, slip next 2 sts on a cable needle and leave at back of work, k2, then k2 from cable needle.

C4F = cable 4 front, slip next 2 sts on a cable needle and leave at front of work, k2, then k2 from cable needle.

Cr3R = cross 3 right, knit into front of 3rd st on left-hand needle, then into front of 2nd stitch on left-hand needle, then into first st and slip all 3 sts off left-hand needle together.

MB = make bobble, [k1, p1, k1] all into next st, turn, p3, turn, k3, turn, p3, turn, sk2p.

See also page 134.

Note

When working from Chart, odd numbered rows are knit rows and read from right to left. Even numbered rows are purl rows and read from left to right.

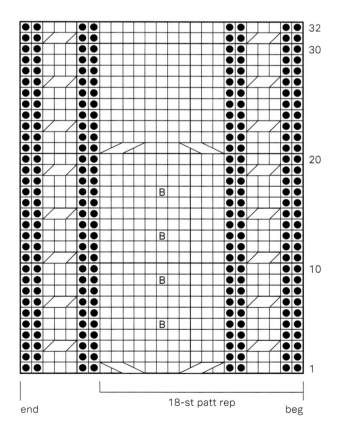

end

18-st patt rep

beg

KEY

☐ K on RS, P on WS

● P on RS, K on WS

B MB

Cr3R

C4B

C4F

Back

Using size 3 (3.25mm) needles, cast on 119(135:151) sts.

Row 1 (RS) P2, k3, p2, [k9, p2, k3, p2] to end.

Row 2 K2, p3, k2, [p9, k2, p3, k2] to end.

Row 3 As row 1.

Row 4 K2, p3, k2, [p3, M1, p3, M1, p3, k2, p3, k2] to end. *133(151:169) sts*

Work in patt from Chart.

Row 1 (RS) [P2, k3, p2, C4B, k3, C4F] tp last 7 sts, p2, k3, p2.

Row 2 K2, p3, k2, [p11, k2, p3, k2] to end.

These 2 rows set the patt.

Work even until back measures 3in/8cm from cast-on edge.

Change to size 2–3 (3mm) needles.

Work a further 3in/8cm.

Change to size 3 (3.25mm) needles.

Work even until back measures 14¼(14½:15)in/ 36(37:38)cm from cast-on edge, ending with a wrong side row.

Shape armholes

Bind off 10(12:14) sts at beg of next 2 rows. *113(127:141) sts*

Next row K1, skp, patt to last 3 sts, k2tog, k1.

Next row P1, p2tog, patt to last 3 sts, p2tog tbl, p1.

Rep the last 2 rows 1(2:3) time(s) more. *105(115:125) sts*

Next row K1, skp, patt to last 3 sts, k2tog, k1.

Next row Patt to end.

Rep the last 2 rows 5(6:7) times more. *93(101:109) sts*

Work even until back measures 22(22¾:23½)in/ 56(58:60)cm from cast-on edge, ending with a wrong side row.

Shape shoulders

Bind off 10(11:12) sts at beg of next 4 rows.

Leave the rem 53(57:61) sts on a spare needle.

Front

Work as given for back until front measures 18½19:19¼)in/47(48:49)cm from cast-on edge, ending with a wrong side row.

Shape front neck

Next row Patt 30(33:36) turn and work on these sts for first side of neck.

Dec one st at neck edge on every right side row until 20(22:24) sts rem.

Work even until front measures the same as back to shoulder, ending at armhole edge.

Shape shoulder

Next row Bind off 10(11:12) sts, patt to end.

Patt 1 row.

Bind off rem 10(11:12) sts.

With right side facing, rejoin yarn to rem sts, place center 33(37:41) sts on a holder, rejoin yarn to rem sts, patt to end.

Dec one st at neck edge on every right side row until 20(22:24) sts rem.

Work even until front measures the same as back to shoulder, ending at armhole edge.

Shape shoulder

Next row Bind off 10(11:12) sts, patt to end.

Patt 1 row.

Bind off rem 10(11:12) sts.

Sleeves

Using size 2–3 (3mm) needles, cast on 87(103:119) sts.

Row 1 (RS) P2, k3, p2, [k9, p2, k3, p2] to end.

Row 2 K2, p3, k2, [p9, k2, p3, k2] to end.

Row 3 As row 1.

Row 4 K2, p3, k2, [p3, M1, p3, M1, p3, k2, p3, k2] to end. *97(115:133) sts*

Change to size 3 (3.25mm) needles.

Work in patt from Chart.

Row 1 (RS) [P2, k3, p2, C4B, k3, C4F] to last 7 sts, p2, k3, p2.

Row 2 K2, p3, k2, [p11, k2, p3, k2] to end.

These 2 rows set the patt.

Work even until sleeve measures 6in/15cm from cast-on edge, ending with a wrong side row.

Shape top

Bind off 10(12:14) sts at beg of next 2 rows.

77(91:105) sts

Next row K1, skp, patt to last 3 sts, k2tog, k1.

Next row Patt to end.

Rep the last 2 rows until 39(49:59) sts rem, ending with a wrong side row.

Dec one st at each end of next 6(8:10) rows.

27(33:39) sts

Bind off 3 sts at beg on next 4 rows.

Bind off.

Neckband

Join right shoulder seam.

With right side facing, size 2–3 (3mm) needles, pick up and k30(35:37) sts down left side of front neck k33(37:41) from front neck holder, pick up and k30(33:36) sts up right side of front neck, k53(57:61) from back neck holder. *146(160:174) sts*

Rib row [K1, p1] to end.

Rep the last row 9 times.

Bind off in rib.

Finishing

Join left shoulder and neckband seam. Work embroidered flowers using five-petaled lazy daisy stitch and a French knot in the center in a contrasting color (see page 133), along the edge of the sleeves and hem, as shown. Add single lazy daisy stitches in green yarn, as shown. Join side and sleeve seams. Sew in sleeves.

Blossom socks

Knitted with the same pattern as the blossom sweater, these socks are both cozy for wearing around the house and really pretty, too.

Finished size
To fit shoe size US 6–8(9–10)/UK 4–6(7–8)

Yarns
Rowan *Wool Cotton 4ply*
2 x 1¾oz/197yd balls in Flower 485
Small amounts in Leaf 491, Violet 490, and Antique 480 for embroidery

Needles
Pair each of size 2 (2.75mm) and size 3 (3.25mm) knitting needles
Cable needle

Extras
Stitch markers

Gauge
28 sts and 36 rows to 4in/10cm measured over St st using size 3 (3.25mm) needles, *or size to obtain correct gauge.* 30 sts and 37 rows to 4in/10cm measured over patt using size 3 (3.25mm) needles, *or size to obtain correct gauge.*

Abbreviations
C4B = cable 4 back, slip next 2 sts on a cable needle and leave at back of work, k2, then k2 from cable needle.
C4F = cable 4 front, slip next 2 sts on a cable needle and leave at front of work, k2, then k2 from cable needle.
Cr3R = cross 3 right, knit into front of 3rd st on left-hand needle, then into front of 2nd stitch on left-hand needle, then into first st and slip all 3 sts off left-hand needle together.
MB = make bobble, [k1, p1, k1] all into next st, turn, p3, turn, k3, turn, p3, turn, sk2p.

See also page 134.

Note

When working from Chart, odd numbered rows are knit rows and read from right to left. Even numbered rows are purl rows and read from left to right.

To make

Using size 2 (2.75mm) needles, cast on 72 sts.
Distribute sts evenly on 3 needles.
1st round [P2, k3, p2, k11] 4 times.
Rep 1st round 3 times more.
Change to size 3 (3.25mm) needles.
1st round [P2, k3, p2, C4B, k3, C4F] 4 times.
2nd to 4th rounds [P2, k3, p2, k11] 4 times.
These 4 rounds set the patt.
Work a further 50 rounds, from Chart, noting that all rounds are right side rows.

Back heel shaping

Change to size 2 (2.75mm) needles.
1st row K17, turn.
2nd row Sl 1, p28, turn.
3rd row Sl 1, k28, turn.
Work on these 29 sts, arrange rem sts on two needles.
Rep the last 2 rows 14 times more, ending with a knit row.

Heel shaping

Next row Sl 1, p15, p2tog, p1, turn.
Next row Sl 1, k4, skp, k1, turn.
Next row Sl 1, p5, p2tog, p1, turn.
Next row Sl 1, k6, skp, k1, turn.
Cont in this way, working one more st on every row until all the sts from back heel have been worked, do not turn. *17 sts*

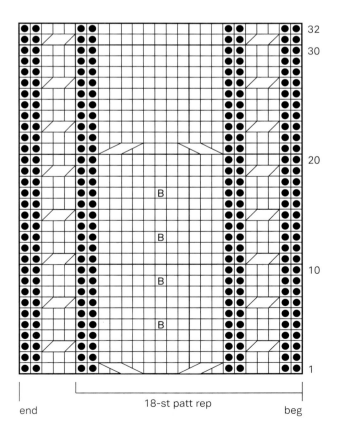

18-st patt rep

end   beg

KEY

☐ K on RS, P on WS

● P on RS, K on WS

B MB

Cr3R

C4B

C4F

Foot shaping

With right side facing, pick up and k15 sts along side of back heel, place a marker, patt 43 sts from needles, place a marker, pick up and k15 sts along other side of heel flap. *90 sts*

Arrange these sts evenly on 3 needles.

1st round Knit to within 3 sts of marker, k2tog, k1, slip marker, patt to next marker, slip marker, k1, skp, knit to end.

Keeping center 43 sts in patt, work as foll:

2nd round Patt to end.

Rep the last 2 rounds 14(8) times more. *60(72) sts*

Cont in rounds until work measures 8(8 ½)in/20(22)cm or length from back of heel to beg of toes.

Cont in St st.

Toe shaping

1st round Knit to within 3 sts of marker, k2tog, k1, slip marker, k1, skp, knit to within 3 sts of next marker, k2tog, k1, slip marker, k1, skp, knit to end.

2nd round Knit to end.

Rep the last 2 rounds until 24(32) sts rem.

Slip first 6(8) sts onto one needle, next 12(16) sts onto another needle, and rem 6(8) sts onto end of first needle.

Fold sock inside out and bind one st from each needle off together. Work embroidered flowers using five-petaled lazy daisy stitch and a French knot in the center in a contrasting color (see page 133), along the top edge of the sock, as shown. Add single lazy daisy stitches in green yarn, as shown.

Blossom fingerless gloves

Enjoy these in the same way as the blossom socks. They are both pretty and practical, as they are cozy to wear but give you the freedom to use your fingers.

Finished size
To fit an average-sized hand

Yarns
Rowan *Wool Cotton 4ply*
2 x 1¾oz/197yd balls in Flower 485
Small amounts in Leaf 491, Violet 490, and Antique 480 for embroidery

Needles
Pair each of size 2 (2.75mm), size 2–3 (3mm), and size 3 (3.25mm) knitting needles
Cable needle

Gauge
28 sts and 36 rows to 4in/10cm measured over St st using size 3 (3.25mm) needles, *or size to obtain correct gauge.* 30 sts and 37 rows to 4in/10cm measured over patt using size 3 (3.25mm) needles, *or size to obtain correct gauge.*

Abbreviations
C4B = cable 4 back, slip next 2 sts on a cable needle and leave at back of work, k2, then k2 from cable needle.
C4F = cable 4 front, slip next 2 sts on a cable needle and leave at front of work, k2, then k2 from cable needle.
Cr3R = cross 3 right, knit into front of 3rd st on left-hand needle, then into front of 2nd stitch on left-hand needle, then into first st and slip all 3 sts off left-hand needle together.
MB = make bobble, [k1, p1, k1] all into next st, turn, p3, turn, k3, turn, p3, turn, sk2p.
See also page 134.

Note

When working from Chart, odd numbered rows are knit rows and read from right to left. Even numbered rows are purl rows and read from left to right.

To make

LEFT GLOVE

Using size 2 (2.75mm) needles, cast on 82 sts.

1st row P2, [k3, p3, k11, p3] 4 times.

2nd row [K3, p11, k3, p3] 4 times, k2.

These 2 rows set the patt.

3rd and 4th rows As 1st and 2nd rows.

Change to size 3 (3.25mm) needles.

Work in patt from Chart.

1st row P2, [k3, p3, C4B, k3, C4F, p3] 4 times.

2nd row [K3, p11, k3, p3] 4 times, k2.

These 2 rows set the patt.

Work a further 49 rows.

Dec row [K1, k2tog, p11, k1, k2tog, p3] 4 times, k2.

74 sts

Cont in patt as set.

** Work a further 14 rows.

Thumb shaping

1st row P2, M1, patt to last 2 sts, M1, p2.

2nd row K2, p1, patt to last 3 sts, p1, k2.

3rd row P2, k1, M1, patt to last 3 sts, M1, k1, p2.

4th row K2, p2, patt to last 4 sts, p2, k2.

5th row P2, k2, M1, patt to last 4 sts, M1, k2, p2.

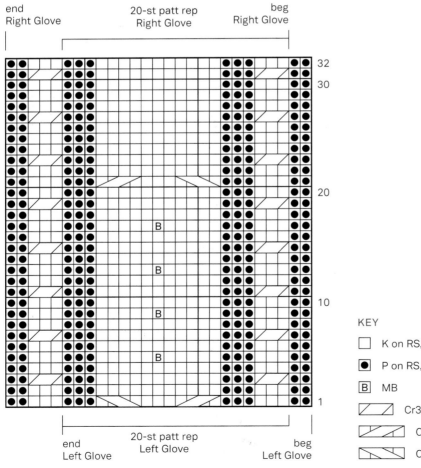

end
Right Glove

20-st patt rep
Right Glove

beg
Right Glove

end
Left Glove

20-st patt rep
Left Glove

beg
Left Glove

KEY

☐ K on RS, P on WS

● P on RS, K on WS

B MB

Cr3R

C4B

C4F

6th row K2, p3, patt to last 5 sts, p3, k2.

Cont in this way, inc one st on every right side row until the foll row has been worked.

17th row P2, k8, M1, patt to last 10 sts, M1, k8, p2.

18th row K2, p9, patt to last 11 sts, p9, k2.

19st row P2, k8, turn, and work on these sts for thumb. Work 9 rows as set. Bind off.

19th row With right side facing, rejoin yarn to next st, patt to last 10 sts, k8, p2.

20th row K2, p8, turn, and work on these sts for thumb. Work 9 rows as set. Bind off.

Next row With wrong side facing, rejoin yarn to next st, patt to end.

Work a further 10 rows in patt, ending with a 32nd row.

Change to size 2–3 (3mm) needles.

Work 6 rows in patt. Bind off.

RIGHT GLOVE

Using size 2 (2.75mm) needles, cast on 82 sts.

1st row [P3, k11, p3, k3] 4 times, p2.

2nd row K2, [p3, k3, p11, k3] 4 times.

These 2 rows set the patt.

3rd and 4th rows As 1st and 2nd rows.

Change to size 3 (3.25mm) needles.

Work in patt from Chart.

1st row [P3, C4B, k3, C4F, p3, k3] 4 times, p2.

2nd row K2, [p3, k3, p11, k3] 4 times.

These 2 rows set the patt.

Work a further 49 rows.

Dec row K2, [p3, k2tog, k1, p11, k2tog, k1] 4 times.

74 sts

Cont in patt as set.

Work as given for Left Glove from ** to end.

Finishing

Work embroidered flowers using five-petaled lazy daisy stitch and a French knot in the center in a contrasting color (see page 133), along the top edge of the glove, as shown. Add single lazy daisy stitches in green yarn, as shown. Join side and thumb seams.

Bloom brooch

This pretty, simple, asymmetric flowery brooch can be knitted in several toning or contrasting colors to make an eye-catching statement. Add the brooch, or brooches, to a plain summer frock or top.

Finished size
Approx 3in/8cm wide by 3in/8cm deep

Yarn
Small amount of Rowan *Pure Wool DK* in color of your choice

Needles
Pair of size 3 (3.25mm) knitting needles

Extras
One button
One brooch back

Abbreviations
See page 134.

Flower
Each flower is made up of an outer, a middle, and a center in the same color

Outer flower piece
Using size 3 (3.25mm) needles, cast on 110 sts.
Row 1 (WS) Knit to end.
Row 2 [K1, bind off 20 sts] 5 times. *10 sts on needle*
Leaving a long end, break off yarn, thread through rem sts, draw up very tightly to form flower shape and secure, then with right side facing bring yarn through to center.

Center flower piece
Using size 3 (3.25mm) needles, cast on 80 sts.
Row 1 (WS) Knit to end.
Row 2 [K1, bind off 14 sts] 5 times. *10 sts on needle*
Leaving a long end, break off yarn, thread through rem sts, draw up very tightly to form flower shape and secure, then with right side facing bring yarn of outer through to center of middle flower.

Inner flower piece

Using size 3 (3.25mm) needles, cast on 50 sts.

Row 1 (WS) Knit to end.

Row 2 [K1, bind off 8 sts] 5 times. *10 sts on needle*
Leaving a long end, break off yarn, thread through
rem sts, draw up very tightly to form flower shape and
secure, then with right side facing bring yarn of outer
and middle through to center of inner flower.

Finishing

Secure all 3 pieces together.

Sew a button to center and a brooch back to back.

Bloom bag

A simple tote bag, knitted in stockinette stitch and lined with a pretty striped knitted fabric, is adorned front and back with a veritable garden of bloom flowers in a range of colors.

Finished size
Approx 10in/25cm wide by 10¼in/26cm deep

Yarns
Rowan *Pure Wool DK*
3 x 1¾oz/123yd balls in Enamel 013 (MC)
2 x 1¾oz/123yd balls each in Hyacinth 026 (A), Ultra 55 (B), Pier 006 (C), and Avocado 019 (D)

Needles
Pair of size 3 (3.25mm) knitting needles

Extras
27½in/70cm of 1½-in/4-cm wide petersham ribbon
32 buttons

Gauge
24 sts and 32 rows to 4in/10cm measured over St st using size 3 (3.25mm) needles, *or size to obtain correct gauge.*

Abbreviations
See page 134.

Outer
BACK and FRONT (both alike)
Using size 3 (3.25mm) needles and MC, cast on 60 sts.
Knit 5 rows.
Beg with a knit row, work in St st until piece measures 10¼in/26cm from cast-on edge, ending with a purl row.
Bind off.

GUSSET (make 2 pieces)
Using size 3 (3.25mm) needles, cast on 12 sts.
Knit 5 rows.
Beg with a knit row, work in St st until piece measures

10 ¼in/26cm from cast-on edge, ending with a purl row.
Mark each end of last row with a colored thread.
Beg with a knit row, cont in St st until work fits halfway along bound-off edge of outer piece—40 rows.
Bind off.

HANDLES (make 2)
Using size 3 (3.25mm) needles, cast on 21 sts.
Next row K5, sl 1pw, k9, sl 1pw, k5.
Next row Purl to end.
Rep the last 2 rows until handle measures 16in/40cm, ending with a purl row.
Bind off.

FLOWERS (make 8 in each color A, B, C, and D)
Each flower is made up of an outer, a middle, and a center in the same color.
Outer flower piece
Using size 3 (3.25mm) needles, cast on 110 sts.
Row 1 (WS) Knit to end.
Row 2 [K1, bind off 20 sts] 5 times. *10 sts on needle*
Leaving a long end, break off yarn, thread through rem sts, draw up very tightly to form flower shape and secure, then with right side facing bring yarn through to center.
Center flower piece
Using size 3 (3.25mm) needles, cast on 80 sts.
Row 1 (WS) Knit to end.
Row 2 [K1, bind off 14 sts] 5 times. *10 sts on needle*
Leaving a long end, break off yarn, thread through rem sts, draw up very tightly to form flower shape and secure, then with right side facing bring yarn of outer through to center of middle flower.
Inner flower piece
Using size 3 (3.25mm) needles, cast on 50 sts.
Row 1 (WS) Knit to end.
Row 2 [K1, bind off 8 sts] 5 times. *10 sts on needle*
Leaving a long end, break off yarn, thread through rem sts, draw up very tightly to form flower shape and secure, then with right side facing bring yarn of outer

and middle through to center of inner flower.
To complete
Secure all 3 pieces together.

Lining
BACK and FRONT (both alike)
Using size 3 (3.25mm) needles and A, cast on 56 sts.
Beg with a knit row, work in St st and stripe patt 2 rows each A, B, C, and D, until piece measures 10in/25cm from cast-on edge, ending with a purl row.
Bind off.

GUSSET (make 2 pieces)
Using size 3 (3.25mm) needles, cast on 10 sts.
Beg with a knit row, work in St st and stripe patt 2 rows each A, B, C, and D, until piece measures 10in/25cm from cast-on edge, ending with a purl row.
Mark each end of last row with a colored thread.
Beg with a knit row, cont in St st until work fits halfway along bound-off edge of lining.
Bind off.

Finishing
Outer
Join bound-off edges of gussets.
Using a button, secure flowers to front and back.
Sew row ends of gusset to row ends and cast-on edges of back and front.

Lining
Make up lining in same way.
With wrong sides together, place lining inside bag.
Join lining to last row of garter-st edging.
Place petersham ribbon along center of wrong side of handle and slip st in place along knitted slipped sts. Bring row ends of handle together encasing petersham ribbon and sew row ends together to form seam.
Sew on handles.

Herbaceous pillow

This is the enthusiastic knitter's project, par excellence. Lovely, different-textured designs combine in knitted squares to make a show-stopping pillow that looks good in almost any setting.

Finished size
To fit a 16in/40cm square pillow form

Yarn
5 x 1¾oz/123yd balls of Rowan *Wool Cotton* in Antique 900

Needles
Pair of size 5 (3.75mm) knitting needles

Extras
16in/40cm square pillow form

Gauge
22 sts and 30 rows to 4in/10cm measured over rev St st using size 5 (3.75mm) needles, *or size to obtain correct gauge.*

Abbreviations
M1p = make one st purlwise, pick up the bar lying between the sts and purl into the back of it.
MK = make knot, [k1, p1, k1, p1, k1] all in next st, turn, p5, turn and pass 2nd, 3rd, 4th and 5th sts (one at a time) over the 1st st and off the needle, then knit into the back of this st.
MB = make bobble, [k1, p1, k1, p1, k1] all in next st, turn, p5, turn, k5, turn, p2tog, p1, p2tog, turn, sk2p. See also page 134.

Note
When working from Charts, odd numbered rows are right side rows and read from right to left. Even numbered rows are wrong side rows and read from left to right.

Chart A – Square 1

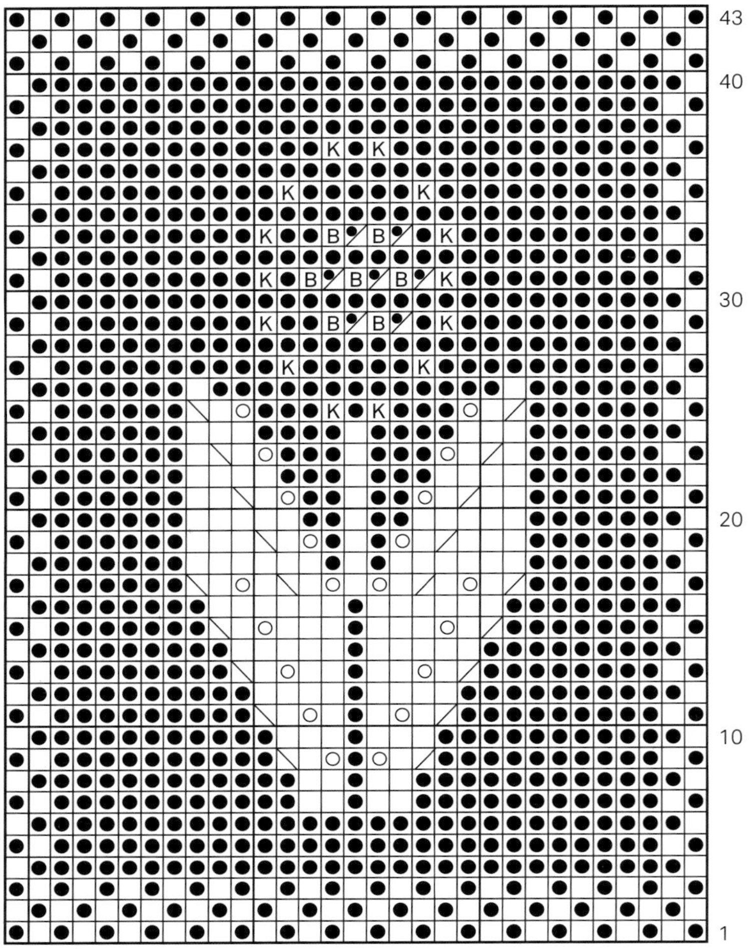

Chart B – Square 2

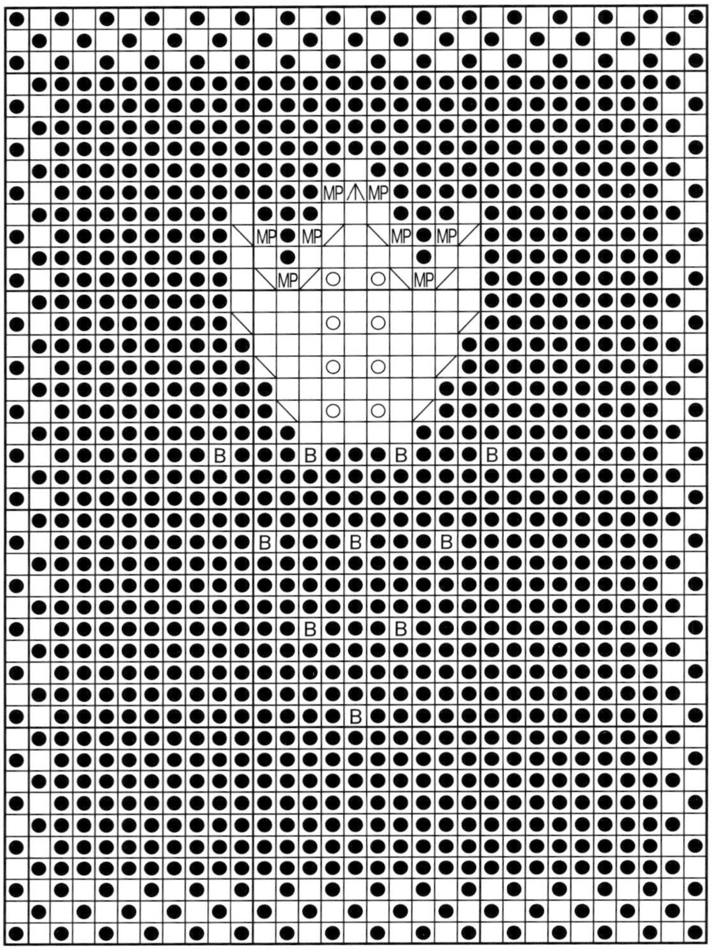

KEY

☐ K on RS, P on WS

● P on RS, K on WS

◿ K2tog

◺ Skp

◿ P2tog

△ S2kp

○ Yon

MP M1p

B MB

K MK

Square 1 (make 9)

Using size 5 (3.75mm) needles and leaving a 8in/20cm end, cast on 31 sts.

Rows 1 to 3 P1, [k1, p1] to end.

Row 4 P1, knit to last st, p1.

Row 5 P1, k1, purl to last 2 sts, k1, p1.

These 2 rows form the rev St st with seed st borders.

Working from row 6 of Chart A, complete the square.

Leaving a 8in/20cm end, bind off in seed st.

Square 2

As Square 1 but work from Chart B.

Finishing

Alternating squares 1 and 2, join 9 squares together to form a larger square 3 squares wide by 3 squares long. With right sides together, sew 3 sides together. Turn to right side. Insert pillow form, join remaining seam.

Herbaceous throw

The perfect complement to the Herbaceous pillow, this throw will look stunning over a sofa or as a finishing touch at the end of a bed.

Finished size
37in/ 94cm by 47¾in/121cm

Yarn
18 x 1¾oz/123yd balls of Rowan *Wool Cotton* in Antique 900

Needles
Pair of size 5 (3.75mm) knitting needles

Gauge
22 sts and 30 rows to 4in/10cm measured over rev St st using size 5 (3.75mm) needles, *or size to obtain correct gauge.*

Abbreviations
M1p = make one st purlwise, pick up the bar lying between the sts and purl into the back of it.

MK = make knot, [k1, p1, k1, p1, k1] all in next st, turn, p5, turn and pass 2nd, 3rd, 4th, and 5th sts (one at a time) over the 1st st and off the needle, then knit into the back of this st.

MB = make bobble, [k1, p1, k1, p1, k1] all in next st, turn, p5, turn, k5, turn, p2tog, p1, p2tog, turn, sk2p. See also page 134.

Note
When working from Charts, odd numbered rows are right side rows and read from right to left. Even numbered rows are wrong side rows and read from left to right.

Square 1 (make 32)
Using size 5 (3.75mm) needles and leaving a 8in/20cm end, cast on 31 sts.

Rows 1 to 3 P1, [k1, p1] to end.

Row 4 P1, knit to last st, p1.

Chart A – Square 1

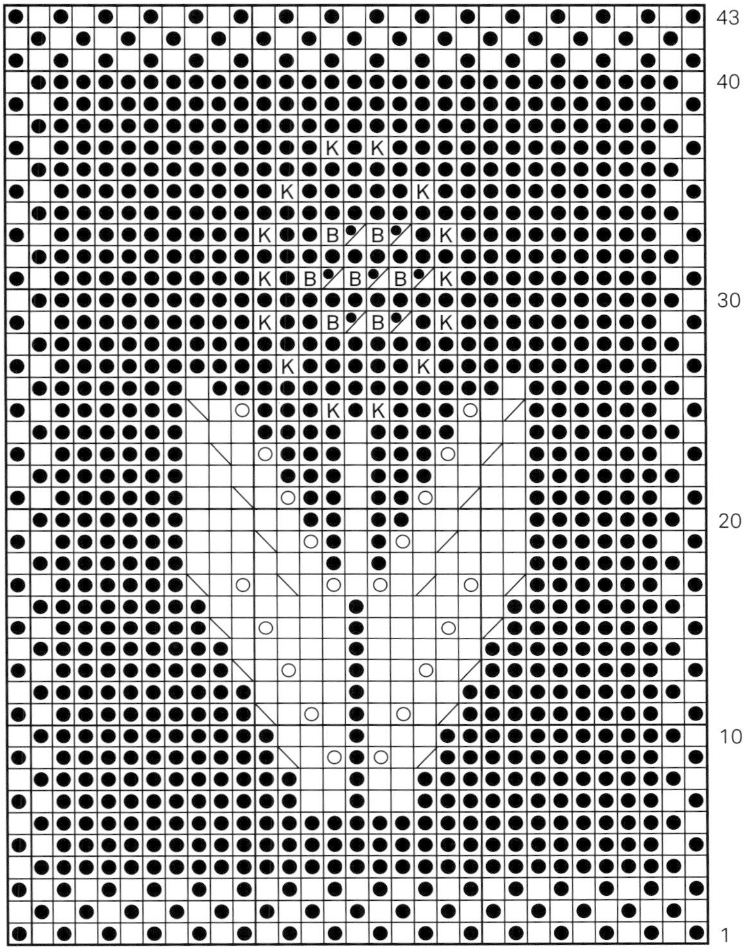

Chart B – Square 2

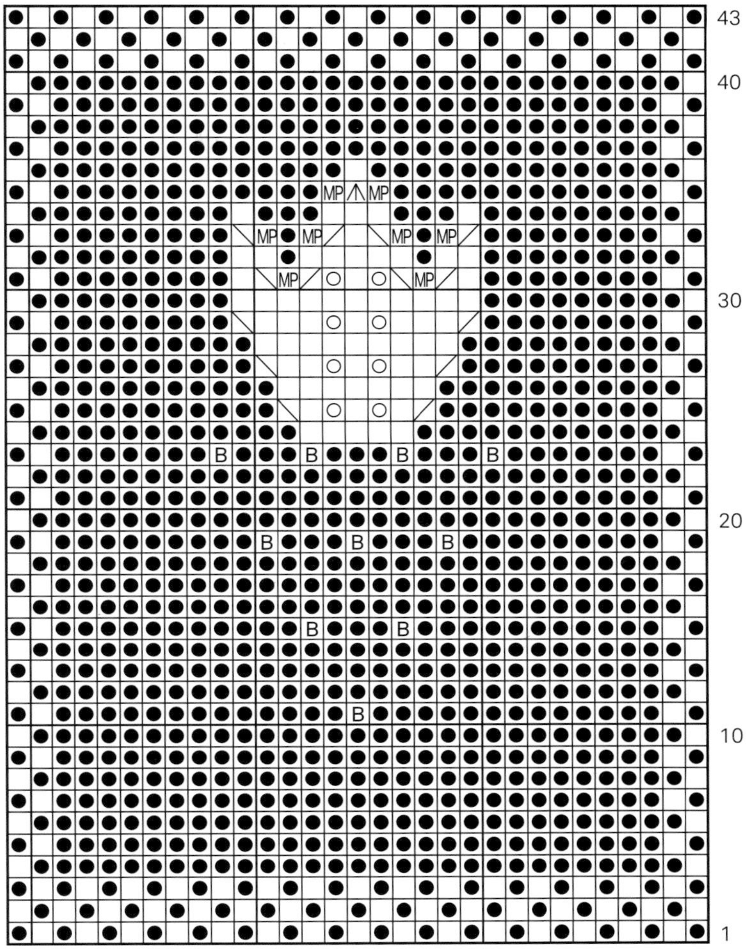

KEY

□	K on RS, P on WS
●	P on RS, K on WS
⧄	K2tog
⧅	Skp
⬛	P2tog
⋀	S2kp
○	Yon
MP	M1p
B	MB
K	MK

Row 5 P1, k1, purl to last 2 sts, k1, p1.

These 2 rows form the rev St st with seed st borders.

Working from row 6 of Chart A, complete the square.

Leaving a 8in/20cm end, bind off in seed st.

Square 2 (make 31)

As Square 1 but work from Chart B.

Finishing

Alternating squares 1 and 2, with square 1 in each corner, join squares together to form a throw 7 squares wide by 9 squares long.

Fleur cardigan

This neatly shaped, crossover front cardigan, with its delicate flower design around the hem, is really versatile. It looks good worn with a casual top and pants, but would also dress up with a fitted skirt.

Finished size

To fit bust

32	34	36	38	40	42	44	in
82	86	92	97	102	107	112	cm

ACTUAL MEASUREMENTS

Bust

33	35½	37¾	39¼	42	44½	46¾	in
84	90	96	101	107	113	119	cm

Length to shoulder

22	22½	23	23¼	23¾	24	24½	in
56	57	58	59	60	61	62	cm

Sleeve length

2in/5cm

Yarns

Rowan *Wool Cotton 4ply*
7(7:8:8:9:9:10) x 1¾oz/197yd balls in Aqua 487 (MC)
1 x 1¾oz/197yd ball in Leaf 491

Needles

Pair each of size 2–3 (3mm) and size 3 (3.25mm) knitting needles

Extras

One small button

Gauge

28 sts and 36 rows to 4in/10cm measured over St st using size 3 (3.25mm) needles, *or size to obtain correct gauge.*

Note

When working from Chart, odd numbered rows are knit rows and read from right to left. Even numbered rows are purl rows and read from left to right. When working in pattern, strand yarn not in use loosely across wrong side of work to keep fabric elastic.

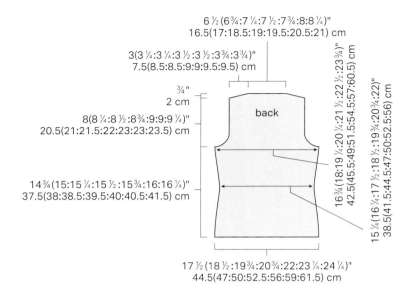

6 ½ (6¾:7 ¼:7 ½:7¾:8:8 ¼)"
16.5(17:18.5:19:19.5:20.5:21) cm

3(3 ¼:3 ¼:3 ½:3 ½:3¾:3¾)"
7.5(8.5:8.5:9:9:9.5:9.5) cm

¾"
2 cm

back

8(8 ¼:8 ½:8¾:9:9:9 ¼)"
20.5(21:21.5:22:23:23:23.5) cm

16¾(18:19 ¼:20 ¼:21 ½:22 ½:23¾)"
42.5(45.5:49:51.5:54.5:57:60.5) cm

14¾(15:15 ¼:15 ½:15¾:16:16 ¼)"
37.5(38:38.5:39.5:40:40.5:41.5) cm

15 ¼(16 ¼:17 ½:18 ½:19¾:20¾:22)"
38.5(41.5:44.5:47:50:52.5:56) cm

17 ½ (18 ½:19¾:20¾:22:23 ¼:24 ¼)"
44.5(47:50:52.5:56:59:61.5) cm

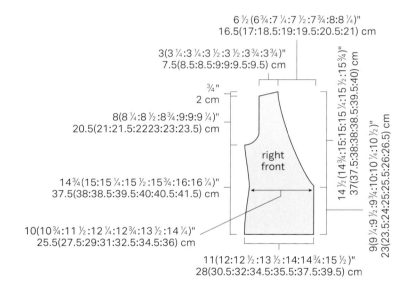

6 ½ (6¾:7 ¼:7 ½:7¾:8:8 ¼)"
16.5(17:18.5:19:19.5:20.5:21) cm

3(3 ¼:3 ¼:3 ½:3 ½:3¾:3¾)"
7.5(8.5:8.5:9:9:9.5:9.5) cm

¾"
2 cm

8(8 ¼:8 ½:8¾:9:9:9 ¼)"
20.5(21:21.5:2223:23:23.5) cm

right
front

14½:14¾:15:15 ¼:15 ½:15¾)"
37(37.5:38:38.5:38.5:39.5:40) cm

14¾(15:15 ¼:15 ½:15¾:16:16 ¼)"
37.5(38:38.5:39.5:40:40.5:41.5) cm

9(9 ½:9 ½:9¾:10:10 ¼:10 ½)"
23(23.5:24:25:25.5:26:26.5) cm

10(10¾:11 ½:12 ¼:12¾:13 ½:14 ¼)"
25.5(27.5:29:31:32.5:34.5:36) cm

11(12:12 ½:13 ½:14:14¾:15 ½)"
28(30.5:32:34.5:35.5:37.5:39.5) cm

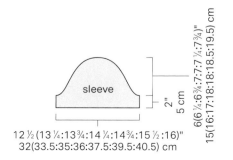

sleeve

6(6 ¼:6¾:7:7 ¼:7¾)"
15(16:17:18:18.5:19.5) cm

2"
5 cm

12 ½ (13 ¼:13¾:14 ¼:14¾:15 ½:16)"
32(33.5:35:36:37.5:39.5:40.5) cm

Abbreviations

See page 134.

Back

Using size 2–3 (3mm) needles and MC, cast on
121(129:137:145:153:161:169) sts.
Rib row 1 (RS) K1, [p1, k1] to end.
Rib row 2 P1, [k1, p1] to end.
Rep the last 2 rows 9 times more, inc one st at center
of last row. *122(130:138:146:154:162:170) sts*
Change to size 3 (3.25mm) needles.
Beg with a knit row, work in St st.
Work 2 rows.
Work in patt from Chart.
Row 1 Patt 6(10:3:7:0:4:8) sts before patt rep, work
across row 1 of 22-st patt rep 5(5:6:6:7:7:7) times,
patt 6(10:3:7:0:4:8) sts after patt rep.
Row 2 Patt 6(10:3:7:0:4:8) sts before patt rep, work
across row 2 of 22-st patt rep 5(5:6:6:7:7:7) times,
patt 6(10:3:7:0:4:8) sts after patt rep.
These 2 rows set the Chart.
Cont to end of row 21.
Cont in MC only.
Work 3 rows.

Dec row K3, skp, knit to last 5 sts, k2tog, k3.
Work 3 rows.
Rep the last 4 rows 6 times more and the dec row
again.
Work 7(9:11:13:15:17:19) rows.
Inc row K3, M1, knit to last 3 sts, M1, k3.
Work 7 rows.
Rep the last 8 rows 4 times more and the inc row
again. *118(126:134:142:150:158:166) sts*
Work 11 rows.

Shape armholes

Bind off 5(6:6:7:7:8:8) sts at beg of next 2 rows.
108(114:122:128:136:142:150) sts
Next row K2, skp, knit to last 4 sts, k2tog, k2.
Next row P2, p2tog, purl to last 4 sts, p2tog tbl, p2.
Rep the last 2 rows 1(1:2:2:3:3:4) time(s) more.
100(106:110:116:120:126:130) sts
Next row K2, skp, knit to last 4 sts, k2tog, k2.
Next row Purl to end.
Rep the last 2 rows 5(6:6:7:7:8:8) times more.
88(92:96:100:104:108:112) sts
Work 54 rows even.

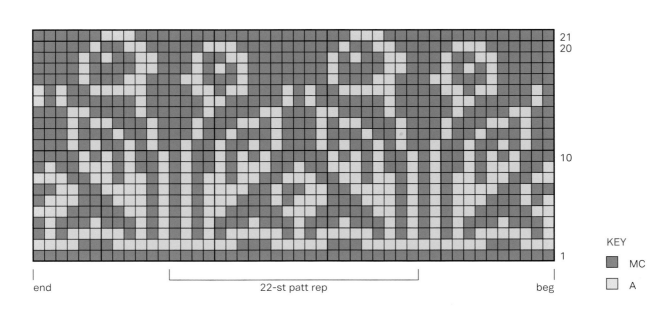

21
20

10

1

| end | 22-st patt rep | beg |

KEY

■ MC
□ A

Shape shoulders

Bind off 7 sts at beg of next 4 rows and
7(8:9:10:11:12:13) sts on foll 2 rows.
Bind off the rem 46(48:50:52:54:56:58) sts.

Left front

Using size 2–3 (3mm) needles and MC, cast on
77(83:87:93:97:103:107) sts.
Rib row 1 (RS) P1, [k1, p1] to end.
Rib row 2 K1, [p1, k1] to end.
Rep the last 2 rows 9 times more, inc one st at center
of last row on **1st, 3rd, 5th, and 7th sizes only**.
78(83:88:93:98:103:108) sts
Change to size 3 (3.25mm) needles.
Beg with a knit row, work in St st.
Work 2 rows.
Work in patt from Chart.
Row 1 Patt 6(10:3:7:0:4:8) sts before patt rep, work
across row 1 of 22-st patt rep 3(3:3:3:4:4:4) times,
patt 6(7:19:20:10:11:12) sts after patt rep.
Row 2 Patt 6(7:19:20:10:11:12) sts before patt rep,
work across row 2 of 22-st patt rep 3(3:3:3:4:4:4)
times, patt 6(10:3:7:0:4:8) sts after patt rep.
These 2 rows set the Chart.
Cont to end of row 21.
Cont in MC only.
Work 3 rows.
Dec row K3, skp, knit to end.
Work 3 rows.
Rep the last 4 rows 6 times more and the dec row
again. *70(75:80:85:90:95:100) sts*
Work 7(9:11:13:15:17:19) rows.

Shape front neck

** **Next row** K3, M1, knit to last 5 sts, k2tog, k3.
Work 1 row.
Next row Knit to last 5 sts, k2tog, k3.
Work 1 row.
Rep the last 2 rows twice more **.
Rep the last 8 rows from ** to ** 4 times more and
the first row again. *55(60:65:70:75:80:85) sts*

Work 1 row.
Next row Knit to last 5 sts, k2tog, k3.
Work 1 row.
Rep the last 2 rows 4 times more.
50(55:60:65:70:75:80) sts

Shape armhole

Next row Bind off 5(6:6:7:7:8:8) sts, knit to end.
45(49:54:58:63:67:72) sts
Next row Purl to end.
Next row K2, skp, knit last 5 sts, k2tog, k3.
Next row Purl to last 4 sts, p2tog tbl, p2.
Rep the last 2 rows 1(1:2:2:3:3:4) time(s) more.
39(43:45:49:51:55:57) sts
Next row K2, skp, knit to last 5 sts, k2tog, k3.
Next row Purl to end.
Rep the last 2 rows 5(6:6:7:7:8:8) times more.
27(29:31:33:35:37:39) sts
2nd, 3rd, 4th, 5th, 6th, and 7th sizes only
Next row Knit to last 5 sts, k2tog, k3.
Work 1 row.
Rep the last 2 rows –(1:3:5:7:9:11) time(s). *27 sts*
1st, 2nd, 3rd, 4th, 5th, and 6th sizes only
Next row Knit to last 5 sts, k2tog, k3.
Work 3 rows.
Rep the last 4 rows 5(4:3:2:1:0:–) time(s) more.
All sizes *21(22:23:24:25:26:27) sts*
Work 30 rows straight.

Shape shoulder

Bind off 7 sts at beg of next and foll right side row.
Work 1 row.
Bind off rem 7(8:9:10:11:12:13) sts.

Right front

Using size 2–3 (3mm) needles and MC, cast on
77(83:87:93:97:103:107) sts.
Rib row 1 (RS) P1, [k1, p1] to end.
Rib row 2 K1, [p1, k1] to end.
Rep the last 2 rows 9 times more, inc one st at center
of last row on **1st, 3rd, 5th, and 7th sizes only**.

78(83:88:93:98:103:108) sts

Change to size 3 (3.25mm) needles.

Beg with a knit row, work in St st.

Work 2 rows.

Work in patt from Chart.

Row 1 Patt 6(7:19:20:10:11:12) sts before patt rep, work across row 1 of 22-st patt rep 3(3:3:3:4:4:4) times, patt 6(10:3:7:0:4:8) sts after patt rep.

Row 2 Patt 6(10:3:7:0:4:8) sts before patt rep, work across row 2 of 22-st patt rep 3(3:3:3:4:4:4) times, patt 6(7:19:20:10:11:12) sts after patt rep.

These 2 rows set the Chart.

Cont to end of row 21.

Cont in MC only.

Work 3 rows.

Dec row Knit to last 5 sts, k2tog, k3.

Work 3 rows.

Rep the last 4 rows 6 times more and the dec row again. *70(75:80:85:90:95:100) sts*

Work 7(9:11:13:15:17:19) rows.

Shape front neck

** Next row K3, skp, knit to last 3 sts, M1, k3.

Work 1 row.

Next row K3, skp, knit to end.

Work 1 row.

Rep the last 2 rows twice more **.

Rep the last 8 rows from ** to ** 4 times more and the first row again. *55(60:65:70:75:80:85) sts*

Work 1 row.

Next row K3, skp, knit to end.

Work 1 row.

Rep the last 2 rows 4 times more and the first row again. *50(55:60:65:70:75:80) sts*

Shape armhole

Next row Bind off 5(6:6:7:7:8:8) sts, purl to end.

45(49:54:58:63:67:72) sts

Next row K3, skp, knit to last 4 sts, k2tog, k2.

Next row P2, p2tog, purl to end.

Rep the last 2 rows 1(1:2:2:3:3:4) time(s) more.

39(43:45:49:51:55:57) sts

Next row K3, skp, knit to last 4 sts, k2tog, k2.

Next row Purl to end.

Rep the last 2 rows 5(6:6:7:7:8:8) times more.

27(29:31:33:35:37:39) sts

2nd, 3rd, 4th, 5th, 6th, and 7th sizes only

Next row K3, skp, knit to end.

Work 1 row.

Rep the last 2 rows –(1:3:5:7:9:11) time(s). *27 sts*

1st, 2nd, 3rd, 4th, 5th, and 6th sizes only

Next row K3, skp, knit to end.

Work 3 rows.

Rep the last 4 rows 5(4:3:2:1:0:–) time(s) more.

All sizes 21(22:23:24:25:26:27) sts

Work 31 rows even.

Shape shoulder

Bind off 7 sts at beg of next and foll wrong side row.

Work 1 row.

Bind off rem 7(8:9:10:11:12:13) sts.

Sleeves

Using size 2–3 (3mm) needles and MC, cast on 88(92:96:100:104:108:112) sts.

Rib row (RS) [K1, p1] to end.

Rep the last row 9 times more.

Change to size 3 (3.25mm) needles.

Beg with a knit row, work in St st.

Work 2 rows.

Work in patt from Chart.

Row 1 Patt 0(2:4:6:8:10:12) sts before patt rep, work across row 1 of 22-st patt rep 4 times, patt 0(2:4:6:8:10:12) sts after patt rep.

Row 2 Patt 0(2:4:6:8:10:12) sts before patt rep, work across row 2 of 22-st patt rep 4 times, patt 0(2:4:6:8:10:12) sts after patt rep.

These 2 rows set the Chart.

Cont to end of row 8.

Shape top

Keeping continuity of patt cont to end of Chart,

then work in MC only, at the same time, bind off 5(6:6:7:7:8:8) sts at beg of next 2 rows.
78(80:84:86:90:92:96) sts

Next row K2, skp, knit to last 4 sts, k2tog, k2.

Next row Purl to end.

Rep the last 2 rows until 34(34:36:36:38:38:40) sts rem, ending on a right(right:wrong:wrong: right:right:wrong) side row.

Dec one st at each end of next 5(5:6:6:7:7:8) rows.
24 sts

Bind off 3 sts at beg of next 4 rows.

Bind off.

Left frontband

Using size 2–3 (3mm) needles and MC, cast on 13 sts.

Rib row 1 (RS) K2, [p1, k1] to last 3 sts, p1, k2.

Rib row 2 K1, [p1, k1] to last 2 sts, p2.

These 2 rows form the rib.

Cont in rib until band fits up left front to center back neck.

Bind off in rib.

Right frontband

Using size 2–3 (3mm) needles and MC, cast on 13 sts.

Rib row 1 (RS) K2, [p1, k1] to last 3 sts, p1, k2.

Rib row 2 P2, [k1, p1] to last st, k1.

These 2 rows form the rib.

Cont in rib until band fits up right front to center back neck.

Bind off in rib.

Buttonhole band

Using size 2–3 (3mm) needles and MC, cast on 13 sts.

Rib row 1 (RS) K2, [p1, k1] to last 3 sts, p1, k2.

Rib row 2 K1, [p1, k1] to end.

These 2 rows form the rib.

Work a further 2 rows.

Buttonhole row K2, p1, k1, p2tog, yo, rib to end.

Cont in rib until band measures 6 ¼(6¾:7:7 ½:8:8 ¼:8¾) in/16(17:18:19:20:21:22)cm from cast-on edge.

Bind off in rib.

Ties (make 2)

Using size 2–3 (3mm)) needles and MC, cast on 13 sts.

Rib row 1 (RS) K2, [p1, k1] to last 3 sts, p1, k2.

Rib row 2 K1, [p1, k1] to end.

These 2 rows form the rib.

Cont in rib until tie measures 23 ½ in/60cm from cast-on edge.

Bind off in rib.

Finishing

Join shoulder seams. Join bound-off edges of front bands, sew in place. Sew bound-off edge of buttonhole band to inner left frontband, level with beg of neck shaping. Join side and sleeve seams. Sew in sleeves. Sew button to inside of right side seam level with neck shaping. Sew one tie to left side seam level with neck shaping. Sew other tie to inner right frontband, level with neck shaping.

Bouquet bag

Another fun project, this little bag, with its spot pattern and appliquéd flowers and leaves, is a show-stopper. The choice of clashing colors gives it even more impact.

Finished size
Approx 10 ¼in/26cm wide by 9 ½in/24cm deep

Yarns
Rowan *Pure Wool DK*
3 x 1¾oz/142yd balls in Avocado 019 (MC)
2 x 1¾oz/142yd balls in Pier 006 (A)
1 x 1¾oz/142yd ball each in Geranium 047 (B), Port 037 (C), Tea Rose 025 (D), and Shamrock 023 (E)

Needles
Pair each of size 3 (3.25mm) and size 6 (4mm) knitting needles

Extras
19¾in/50cm lining fabric
23¾in/60cm of 1 ¼-in/ 3.5-cm wide petersham ribbon
4 buttons
28 small beads

Gauge
22 sts and 30 rows to 4in/10cm measured over St st using size 6 (4mm) needles, *or size to obtain correct gauge.*

Abbreviations
See page 134.

Outer
Back and Front (both alike)
Using size 6 (4mm) needles and MC, cast on 57 sts.
Beg with a knit row, work in St st and patt from Chart A.
Rep rows 1 to 20 three times, then rows 1 to 9 again.
Rows 70 to 73 Using MC, knit to end.
Row 74 Bind off kwise on wrong side.

Chart A – Back and Front

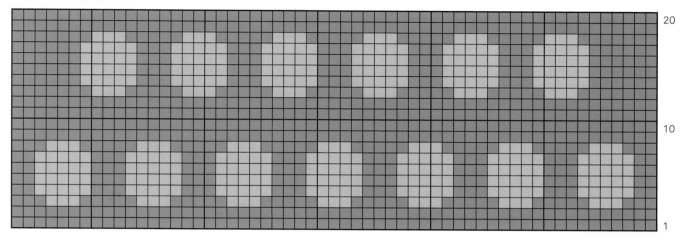

Chart B – Side Gussets

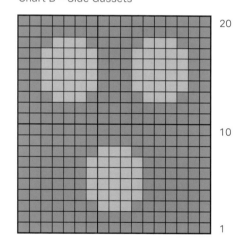

KEY

■ MC

□ A

Side gussets (make 2 pieces)

Using size 6 (4mm) needles and MC, cast on 17 sts.
Beg with a knit row, work in St st and patt from Chart B.
Rep rows 1 to 20 three times, then rows 1 to 9 again.
Rows 70 to 73 Using MC, knit to end.
Row 74 Bind off kwise on wrong side.

Base gusset

Using size 6 (4mm) needles and MC, cast on 17 sts.
Beg with a knit row, work in St st until work fits along cast-on edge of back section.
Bind off.

Handles (make 2)

Using size 6 (4mm) needles and MC, cast on 17 sts.
Next row K4, sl 1pw, k7, sl 1pw, k4.
Next row Purl to end.
Rep the last 2 rows 44 times.
Bind off.

Petal flowers (make 2)

Outer flower piece

Using size 3 (3.25mm) needles and B, cast on 3 sts.
** **Row 1 (RS)** Knit to end.
Row 2 and every alt row Purl to end.
Row 3 K1, [M1, k1] twice.
Row 5 K1, M1, k3, M1, k1.
Row 7 K1, M1, k5, M1, k1.
Row 9 K1, M1, k7, M1, k1.
Row 11 Knit to end.
Row 13 Skp, k7, k2tog.
Row 15 Skp, k5, k2tog.
Row 17 Skp, k3, k2tog. *5 sts* ***

117

Break off yarn and leave sts on the needle.
Onto same needle cast on 3 sts **.
Rep from ** to ** 5 times more, then from ** to ***
once more. *7 petals 35 sts*
Next row [K2tog] 17 times, k1. *18 sts*
Break off yarn, thread through sts, and fasten off
securely.

Inner flower piece
Using size 3 (3.25mm) needles and B, cast on 3 sts.
** Row 1 (RS) Knit to end.
Row 2 and every alt row Purl to end.
Row 3 K1, [M1, k1] twice.
Row 5 K1, M1, k3, M1, k1.
Row 7 K1, M1, k5, M1, k1.
Row 9 Skp, k5, k2tog.
Row 10 P2tog, p3, p2tog tbl. *5 sts ***
Break off yarn and leave sts on the needle.
Onto same needle cast on 3 sts **.
Rep from ** to ** 5 times more, then from ** to ***
once more. *7 petals 35 sts*
Next row [K2tog] 17 times, k1. *18 sts*
Break off yarn, thread through sts, and fasten off
securely.
Sew center of inner flower to center of outer flower.

Loop flowers (make 4)
Outer flower piece
Using size 3 (3.25mm) needles and C, cast on 110 sts.
Row 1 (WS) Knit to end.
Row 2 [K1, bind off 20 sts] 5 times. *10 sts on needle*
Leaving a long end, break off yarn, thread through
rem sts, draw up very tightly to form flower shape and
secure, then with right side facing, bring yarn through
to center.

Center flower piece
Using size 3 (3.25mm) needles and C, cast on 80 sts.
Row 1 (WS) Knit to end.
Row 2 [K1, bind off 14 sts] 5 times.
10 sts on needle

Leaving a long end, break off yarn, thread through
rem sts, draw up very tightly to form flower shape and
secure, then with right side facing, bring yarn of outer
through to center of middle flower.

Inner flower piece
Using size 3 (3.25mm) needles and C, cast on 50 sts.
Row 1 (WS) Knit to end.
Row 2 [K1, bind off 8 sts] 5 times. *10 sts on needle*
Leaving a long end, break off yarn, thread through
rem sts, draw up very tightly to form flower shape and
secure, then with right side facing, bring yarn of outer
and middle through to center of inner flower.

To complete
Secure all 3 pieces together.

Garter flowers (make 4)
Using size 3 (3.25mm) needles and D, cast on 9 sts.
Knit 2 rows.
Row 3 Bind off 6 sts, knit to end. *3 sts*
Row 4 Knit 3.
Row 5 Cast on 6 sts, knit these 6 sts, knit to end.
9 sts
Row 6 Knit to end.
Rep rows 3 to 6 twenty-three times more, then row 3
again. 25 petals completed.
Bind off.
Roll up each flower to form a neat stacked circle and
sew in place.

Elf leaves (make 4)
Using size 3 (3.25mm) needles and E, cast on 5 sts.
Row 1 K1, [sl 1pw, k1] twice.
Row 2 Sl 1pw, [p1, sl1 pw] twice.
Rep the last 2 rows 3 times more for stem.

Main part
Row 1 K2, M1, k1, M1, k2.
Row 2 and every alt row Purl to end.
Row 3 K3, M1, k1, M1, k3.

Row 5 K4, M1, k1, M1, k4.

Row 7 K5, M1, k1, M1, k5.

Row 9 Bind off 3 sts, then k2, M1, k1, M1, k6.

Row 10 Bind off 3 sts, purl to end.

Row 11 to 22 Rep rows 5 to 10 twice.

Rows 23 to 26 Rep rows 5 to 8 once.

Row 27 Bind off 3 sts, knit to end.

Row 28 Bind off 3 sts, purl to end.

Row 29 Skp, k3, k2tog.

Row 30 Purl to end.

Row 31 Skp, k1, k2tog.

Row 32 Purl to end.

Row 33 Sk2p.

Fasten off.

Finishing

Using knitted pieces as templates and adding seam allowance, cut out front, back, sides, and base from lining fabric. Sew ends of base to cast-on edges of sides. Sew row ends of sides to row ends of back and front. Sew base to cast-on edges of back and front. Make up lining in same way.

Place petersham ribbon along center of wrong side of handle and slip st in place along knitted slipped sts. Bring row ends of handle together encasing petersham ribbon and sew row ends together to form seam.

Sew handles to inside of back and front 3in/8cm apart.

Place lining inside bag, fold seam allowance to wrong side, and slip st lining in place.

Sew a button to center of each loop flower. Sew beads to centers of both petal flowers. Sew flowers and leaves to bag as shown in photograph.

Gardenia bolero

This really sweet edge-to-edge bolero makes the perfect accessory for a sleeveless top or dress. Fastened at the front with a ribbon or brooch, it features an unusual cabled and textured pattern interspersed with embroidered yarn flowers.

Finished size

To fit bust

S–M	M–L	L–XL	

ACTUAL MEASUREMENTS

Bust

35	41 ¼	47 ½	in
89	105	121	cm

Length to shoulder

14	15	16	in
35.5	38	40.5	cm

Yarns

4(5:6) x 1¾oz/197yd balls of Rowan *Wool Cotton 4ply* in Violet 490
Small amount of assorted colors for embroidery

Needles

Pair each of size 2 (2.75mm) and size 3 (3.25mm) knitting needles
Circular size 2 (2.75mm) needle
Cable needle

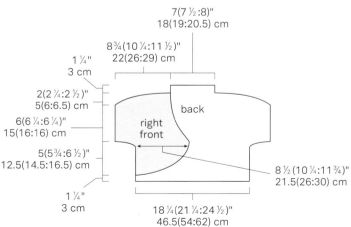

7(7 ½:8)"
18(19:20.5) cm

8¾(10 ¼:11 ½)"
22(26:29) cm

1 ¼"
3 cm

2(2 ¼:2 ½)"
5(6:6.5) cm

6(6 ¼:6 ¼)"
15(16:16) cm

5(5¾:6 ½)"
12.5(14.5:16.5) cm

1 ¼"
3 cm

back

right
front

8 ½ (10 ¼:11 ¾)"
21.5(26:30) cm

18 ¼(21 ¼:24 ½)"
46.5(54:62) cm

Extras

Stitch holders
63in/160cm of ¼in/6mm ribbon

Gauge

30 sts and 35 rows to 4in/10cm measured over patt using size 3 (3.25mm) needles, *or size to obtain correct gauge.*

Abbreviations

C4B = cable 4 back, slip next 2 sts on a cable needle and leave at back of work, k2, then k2 from cable needle.

C4F = cable 4 front, slip next 2 sts on a cable needle and leave at front of work, k2, then k2 from cable needle.

See also page 134.

Back

Using size 2 (2.75mm) needles, cast on 135(159:183) sts.

Seed st row K1, [p1, k1] to end.

Rep this row for 1¼in/3cm, inc one st at center of last row. *136(160:184) sts*

Change to size 3 (3.25mm) needles.

Work in patt.

Row 1 P4, [C4B, C4F, p4] 11(13:15) times.

Row 2 K4, [p8, k4, p1, k1, p1, k1, p1, k1, p2, k4] 5(6:7) times, p8, k4.

Row 3 P4, [k8, p4, k1, p1, k1, p1, k1, p2, k4] 5(6:7) times, k8, p4.

Row 4 K4, [p8, k4, p1, k1, p1, k1, p1, k1, p2, k4] 5(6:7) times, p8, k4.

Rows 5 to 10 Rep rows 3 and 4 three times.

Row 11 P4, [C4B, C4F, p4] 11(13:15) times.

Row 12 K4, [p1, k1, p1, k1, p1, k1, p2, k4, p8, k4] 5(6:7) times, p1, k1, p1, k1, p1, k1, p2, k4.

Row 13 P4, [k1, p1, k1, p1, k1, p1, k2, p4, k8, p4] 5(6:7) times, k1, p1, k1, p1, k1, p1, k2, p4.

Row 14 K4, [p1, k1, p1, k1, p1, k1, p2, k4, p8, k4] 5(6:7) times, p1, k1, p1, k1, p1, k1, p2, k4.

Rows 15 to 20 Rep rows 13 and 14 three times.

These 20 rows form the patt.

Work a further 16(22:28) rows, ending with a wrong side row.

Shape sleeves

Cast on 6 sts at beg of next 8 rows. *184(208:232) sts*

Work even until back measures 12¼(13¼:14)in/ 31.5(33.5:35.5)cm from cast-on edge, ending with a wrong side row.

Shape upper arms

1st row Patt 6 sts, place these 6 sts on a holder, patt to end.

2nd row Patt 6 sts, place these 6 sts on a holder, patt to end.

Rep the last 2 rows 6(7:8) times more.

100(112:124) sts left unworked

Shape shoulders

1st row Patt 12(14:16) sts, place these 12(14:16) sts on a holder, patt to end.

2nd row Patt 12(14:16), place these 12(14:16) sts, on a holder, patt to end.

3rd row Patt 12(14:16) sts, place these 12(14:16) sts on a holder, patt to end.

4th row Patt 12(14:16), place these 12(14:16) sts, on a holder, patt to end.

Place 52(56:60) sts left unworked at center on a size 2 (2.75mm) needle.

Change to size 2 (2.75mm) needles.

Seed st row 1 [K1, p1] to end.

Seed st row 2 [P1, k1] to end.

Rep these 2 rows 6 times more.

Bind off in seed st.

Left front

Using size 3 (3.25mm) needles, cast on 16 sts.

Foundation row (WS) K4, p8, k4.

Work in patt.

Row 1 P4, C4B, C4F, p4.

Row 2 Cast on 3 sts, k1, p2, k4, p8, k4.

Row 3 P4, k8, p4, k1, p1, k1.

Row 4 Cast on 3 sts, [p1, k1] twice, p2, k4, p8, k4.

Row 5 P4, k8, p4, [k1, p1] 3 times.

Row 6 Cast on 3 sts, k1, [p1, k1] 3 times, p2, k4, p8, k4.

Row 7 P4, k8, p4, [k1, p1] 3 times, k2, p1.

Row 8 Cast on 3 sts, k4, [p1, k1] 3 times, p2, k4, p8, k4.

These 8 rows **set** the patt.

Cast on and work into patt 3 sts at beg of 12(16:20) foll wrong side rows. *64(76:88) sts*

Work 4(2:0) rows even, ending with the same patt row as back up to sleeve shaping.

Shape sleeve and front neck

Next row Cast on 6 sts, patt to last 2 sts, work 2 tog.

Next row Patt to end.

Next row Cast on 6 sts, patt to end.

Next row Patt to end.

Rep the last 4 rows once more. *86(98:110) sts*

Keeping armhole edge straight cont to dec at neck edge on every right side row until 66(76:86) sts rem.

Work even until front measures the same as back to upper arm shaping, ending with a wrong side row.

Shape upper arms

Row 1 Patt 6 sts, place these 6 sts on a holder, patt to end.

Row 2 Patt to end.

Rep the last 2 rows 6(7:8) times more.

24(28:32) sts left unworked

Shape shoulder

Row 1 Patt 12(14:16) sts, place these 12(14:16) sts on a holder, patt to end.

Row 2 Patt to end.

Place rem 12(14:16) sts on a holder.

Right front

Using size 3 (3.25mm) needles, cast on 16 sts.

Foundation row (WS) K4, p8, k4.

Work in patt.

Row 1 Cast on 3 sts, k3, p4, C4B, C4F, p4.

Row 2 K4, p8, k4, p1, k1, p1.

Row 3 Cast on 3 sts, [k1, p1] twice, k2, p4, k8, p4.

Row 4 K4, p8, k4, [p1, k1] 3 times.

Row 5 Cast on 3 sts, [p1, k1] 3 times, p1, k2, p4, k8, p4.

Row 6 K4, p8, k4, [p1, k1] 3 times, p2, k1.

Row 7 Cast on 3 sts, p4, [k1, p1] 3 times, k2, p4, k8, p4.

Row 8 K4, p8, k4, [p1, k1] 3 times, p2, k4.

These 8 rows **set** the patt.

Cast on and work into patt 3 sts at beg of 12(16:20) foll right side rows. *64(76:88) sts*

Work 5(3:1) row(s) even, ending with the same patt row as back up to sleeve shaping.

Shape sleeve and front neck

Next row Work 2 tog, patt to end.

Next row Cast on 6 sts, patt to end.

Next row Patt to end.

Next row Cast on 6 sts, patt to end.

Rep the last 4 rows once more. *86(98:110) sts*

Keeping armhole edge straight, cont to dec at neck edge on every right side row until 66(76:86) sts rem.

Work even until front measures the same as back to upper arm shaping, ending with a right side row.

Shape upper arm

Row 1 Patt 6 sts, place these 6 sts on a holder, patt to end.

Row 2 Patt to end.

Rep the last 2 rows 6(7:8) times more.

24(28:32) sts left unworked

Shape shoulder

Row 1 Patt 12(14:16) sts, place these 12(14:16) sts on a holder, patt to end.

Row 2 Patt to end.

Place rem 12(14:16) sts on a holder.

Right frontband

With right side facing, using size 2 (2.75mm) circular
needle, pick up and k64(76:88) sts round curved edge,
then 71(75:79) sts to shoulder.

Seed st row K1, [p1, k1] to end.

Rep the last row 13 times more.

Bind off in seed st.

Left frontband

With right side facing, using size 2 (2.75mm) circular
needle, pick up and k71(75:79) sts to beg of curved
section, then 64(76:88) sts round curved edge.

Seed st row K1, [p1, k1] to end.

Rep the last row 13 times more.

Bind off in seed st.

Sleeve bands

With right sides together, join fronts to back, by
binding off one st from each piece together to form
upper sleeve and shoulder seams.

With right side facing, using size 2 (2.75mm) needles,
pick up and k83(89:95) sts evenly along row ends.

Seed st row K1, [p1, k1] to end.

Rep the last row 6 times more.

Bind off in seed st.

Finishing

Work embroidered flowers using four-petalled lazy
daisy stitch and a French knot in the center in a
contrasting color (see page 133), along the cabled
pattern, as shown.

Join side and underarm seams.

Cut ribbon in half and sew an end to wrong side of
frontband at curved section on each side.

Petal pillow

This round pillow is a flower extravaganza! Like Jacob's coat of many colors, it is made up of as many different colors as you like, gaining its impact from the sizzling mix. The pillow itself is a simple stockinette stitch design to which the flowers are appliquéd.

Finished size
To fit a 18in/50cm round pillow form

Yarns
Rowan *Wool Cotton*
Pillow
5 x 1¾oz/123yd balls in Antique 900 (MC)
Flowers
1 x 1¾oz/123yd ball each in Cypress 968, Tender 951, Windbreak 984, Elf 946, Rich 911, Pier 983, Brolly 980, Café 985, Bilberry 969, and Celadon 979

Needles
Pair each of size 5 (3.75mm) and size 3 (3.25mm) knitting needles

Extras
62 small buttons
18in/50cm round pillow form

Gauge
22 sts and 30 rows to 4in/10cm measured over St st using size 5 (3.75mm) needles, *or size to obtain correct gauge.*

Abbreviations
See page 134.

Pillow cover
Back and Front alike
Using size 5 (3.75mm) needles and MC, cast on 48 sts.
** **1st and 2nd rows** K3, turn, sl 1, purl to end.
3rd and 4th rows K9, turn, sl 1, purl to end.
5th and 6th rows K15, turn, sl 1, purl to end.
7th and 8th rows K21, turn, sl 1, purl to end.
9th and 10th rows K27, turn, sl 1, purl to end.

11th and 12th rows K33, turn, sl 1, purl to end.

13th and 14th rows K39, turn, sl 1, purl to end.

15th and 16th rows K45, turn, sl 1, purl to end.

17th and 18th rows K42, turn, sl 1, purl to end.

19th and 20th rows K36, turn, sl 1, purl to end.

21st and 22nd rows K30, turn, sl 1, purl to end.

23rd and 24th rows K24, turn, sl 1, purl to end.

25th and 26th rows K18, turn, sl 1, purl to end.

27th and 28th rows K12, turn, sl 1, purl to end.

29th and 30th rows K6, turn, sl 1, purl to end.

31st row Knit to end

32nd row Purl to end **.

Rep the last 32 rows 13 times more.

Bind off.

Flowers (make 5 in each of 4 colors and 6 in each of 7 colors, including MC, total 62)

Using size 3 (3.25mm) needles, cast on 57 sts.

Row 1 Purl to end.

Row 2 K2, [k1, slip this st back onto left-hand needle, lift next 8 sts on left-hand needle over this st and off left-hand needle, y2rn, knit st on left-hand needle again, k2) to end. *27 sts*

Row 3 K1, [p2tog, then k1, k1 tbl, k1, k 1tbl all into y2rn, p1] to last st, k1. *32 sts*

Row 4 [K2tog] 16 times.

Break yarn, leaving a long end, thread through rem sts, fasten off securely. Sew row ends of flower together.

Finishing

Secure flowers, with buttons, tightly together onto one side of pillow. Join cast-on and bound-off edges together. Join outside edge three-quarters of the way round. Insert pillow form. Join remainder of seam.

Petal garland

Any extra flowers you make can be strung together to make a little garland to hang on or over a doorway. You can string them on a tube of stockinette stitch, which can be knitted in the round or, if you prefer, on a knitting dolly.

Finished size
Approx 75in/190cm long

Yarns
Rowan *Wool Cotton*
String
1 x 1¾oz/123yd ball in Antique 900
Flowers
Small amount each in Cypress 968, Tender 951, Windbreak 984, Elf 946, Rich 911, Pier 983, Brolly 980, Café 985, Bilberry 969, and Celadon 979

Needles
Pair of double-pointed size 5 (3.75mm) knitting needles
Pair of size 3 (3.25mm) knitting needles

Extras
15 small buttons

Abbreviations
See page 134.

Garland string
Using double-pointed size 5 (3.75mm) needles, cast on 3 sts.
Row 1 [Inc in next st] 3 times. *6 sts*
Do not turn, bring yarn across back of work to beg of row.
Row 2 K6, do not turn, bring yarn across back of work to beg of row.
Rep this row until string measures 75in/190cm.
Work [2tog] 3 times, thread yarn through remaining sts and fasten off.

Flowers (make 15 from 10 colors)
Using size 3 (3.25mm) needles, cast on 57 sts.

Row 1 Purl to end.

Row 2 K2, [k1, slip this st back onto left-hand needle, lift next 8 sts on left-hand needle over this st and off left-hand needle, y2rn, knit st on left-hand needle again, k2] to end. *27 sts*

Row 3 K1, [p2tog, then k1, k1 tbl, k1, k1 tbl all into y2rn, p1] to last st, k1. *32 sts*

Row 4 [K2tog] 16 times.
Break yarn, thread through rem sts, fasten off securely. Sew row ends of flower together.

Finishing

Secure flowers to string with buttons, one each end and the remaining 13 approx 5in/13cm apart.

Poppy brooch

Make a bit of a splash with this big flowery brooch. Pin it on a blouse, on the back pocket of your jeans, or attach it to a tote bag.

Finished size
Approx 4¾in/12cm wide by 4¾in/12cm

Yarns
1 x 1¾oz/123yd ball each of Rowan *Wool Cotton* in Rich 911 (MC) and Antique 900 (A)
Small amount in Inky 908 (B) for embroidery

Needles
Pair of size 5 (3.75mm) knitting needles
Large-eyed yarn needle

Extras
Small amount of filling
Brooch back

Abbreviations
See page 134.

Petals (make 10)
Using size 5 (3.75mm) needles and MC, cast on 7 sts.
Row 1 (RS) Knit to end.
Row 2 Purl to end.
Row 3 K1, M1, knit to last st, M1, k1.
Rows 4 to 7 Rep rows 2 and 3 twice more. *13 sts*
Work 11 rows in St st.
Bind off.

Center (make 2 pieces)
Using size 5 (3.75mm) needles and A, cast on 5 sts.
Row 1 (RS) Knit to end.
Row 2 P1, M1, purl to last st, M1, p1.
Row 3 K1, M1, knit to last st, M1, k1.
Row 4 Purl to end.
Rows 5 and 6 As rows 3 and 4.
Row 7 K1, M1, knit to last st, M1, k1. *13 sts*
Work 6 rows in St st.

Row 14 P1, p2tog, purl to last 3 sts, p2tog tbl, p1.
Row 15 Knit to end.
Rows 16 and 15 As rows 14 and 15.
Row 18 P1, p2tog, purl to last 3 sts, p2tog tbl, p1.
Row 19 K1, skp, knit to last 3 sts, k2tog, k1. *5 sts*
Bind off.

Finishing

Using B and following Chart, duplicate stitch one side
of flower center. Thread a large-eyed yarn needle
with B, bring the needle out to the front at the base of
the stitch to be covered, then insert the needle from
right to left behind the stitch directly above. Insert the
needle from front to back into the base of the stitch
to be covered to complete the duplicate stitch.
Leaving a small gap, sew center back to center front,
stuff lightly, then join gap.
Leaving bound-off edge open, join petals together in
pairs.
Run gathering threads through bound-off edges and
lightly gather, so petals fit round outside edge of
center. Sew in place.
Sew a brooch back to the back.

Flower Center

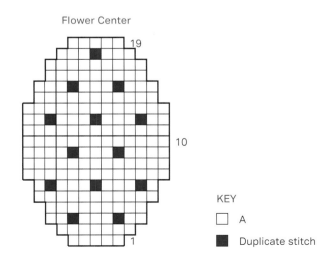

KEY

□ A

■ Duplicate stitch

Poppy brooch

Dahlia bag

This cute shoulder bag sits snugly under your arm, bursting with color and adorned with exuberant blooms. A statement in pink and green, it would also look chic in understated gray and black.

Finished size
Approx 5½in/14cm deep by 10¼in/26cm wide

Yarns
Rowan *Wool Cotton*
3 x 1¾oz/123yd balls in Flower 943 (A)
1 x 1¾oz/123yd ball in Elf 946 (B)

Needles
Pair each of size 3 (3.25mm) and size 5 (3.75mm) knitting needles

Extras
66 beads
23½in/60cm of 1½-in/4-cm wide petersham ribbon
3 snaps

Gauge
24 sts and 32 rows to 4in/10cm measured over St st using size 5 (3.75mm) needles, *or size to obtain correct gauge.*

Abbreviations
See page 134.

Outer
Back and Front (both alike)
Using size 5 (3.75mm) needles and A, cast on 47 sts.
Beg with a knit row, work in St st.
Work 1 row.
Next row P2, inc in next st, purl to last 4 sts, inc in next st, p3.
Next row K2, inc in next st, knit to last 4 sts, inc in next st, k3.
Rep the last 2 rows once more. *55 sts*
Next row Purl to end.
Next row K2, inc in next st, knit to last 4 sts, inc in

next st, k3.

Rep the last 2 rows 3 times more. *63 sts*

Work 34 rows even, ending with a knit row.

Next row (foldline) Knit to end.

Beg with a knit row, work 12 rows in St st.

Bind off.

Gusset and Handle

Using size 5 (3.75mm) needles and A, cast on 11 sts.

Beg with a knit row, work 156 rows in St st, ending with a purl row.

Handle

Cast on 6 sts at beg of next 2 rows. *23 sts*

Next row K6, sl 1pw, k9, sl 1pw, k6.

Next row Purl to end.

Rep the last 2 rows until handle measures 21 ¼ in/54cm, ending with a purl row.

Bind off.

Lining

Back and Front (both alike)

Using size 3 (3.25mm) needles and B, cast on 47 sts.

Beg with a knit row, work in St st.

Work 1 row.

Next row P2, inc in next st, purl to last 4 sts, inc in next st, p3.

Next row K2, inc in next st, knit to last 4 sts, inc in next st, k3.

Rep the last 2 rows once more. *55 sts*

Next row Purl to end.

Next row K2, inc in next st, knit to last 4 sts, inc in next st, k3.

Rep the last 2 rows 3 times more. *63 sts*

Work 22 rows even, ending with a knit row.

Bind off.

Gusset

Using size 3 (3.25mm) needles and A, cast on 11 sts.

Beg with a knit row, work 12 rows in St st.

Break off A, join on B.

Work a further 132 rows.

Break off B, join on A.

Work a further 12 rows.

Bind off.

Flowers (make 3)

Using size 5 (3.75mm) needles and B, cast on 11 sts.

Knit 2 rows.

Row 3 Bind off 8 sts, knit to end. *3 sts*

Row 4 Knit 3.

Row 5 Cast on 8 sts, knit these 8 sts, knit to end. *11 sts*

Row 6 Knit to end.

Row 7 Bind off 8 sts, knit to end. *3 sts*

Rep rows 4 to 7 eight times more. 10 petals completed.

Break off B.

Join on A.

Rep rows 4 to 7 thirty times more. 40 petals completed.

Bind off.

Finishing

Outer

Sew cast-on edge of gusset section to center of bound-off edge of handle section. Sew gusset to sides below foldline. Fold last 12 rows of back and front to wrong side and stitch in place.

Place petersham ribbon along center of wrong side of handle and slip st in place along knitted slipped sts. Bring row ends of handle together, encasing petersham ribbon, and sew row ends together to form seam.

Lining

Leaving first and last 12 rows in A free, sew gusset to sides. With wrong sides together, place lining inside bag, sew bound-off edges together. Sew first and last 12 rows of lining gusset to first 12 rows of bag.

Roll up each flower to form a neat stacked circle and sew in place.

Attach a bead to each end of petals in B, then a further 12 beads at center.

Sew flowers to one side of bag.

Attach snaps to close opening edge.

Useful information

SIZING

The instructions are given for the smallest size, and larger sizes follow in parentheses. If there is only one set of figures, it refers to all sizes. If - (hyphen) or 0 (zero) is given in an instruction for the size you are knitting, then that particular instruction does not apply to your size.

Included with each garment pattern in this book is a size diagram of the finished garment pieces and their dimensions. The size diagram shows the finished width of the garment at the underarm point, and it is this measurement that you should choose first; a useful tip is to measure one of your own garments that is a comfortable fit. Having chosen a size based on width, look at the corresponding length for that size; if you are not happy with the total recommended length, adjust your own garment before beginning your armhole shaping—any adjustment after this point will mean that your sleeve will not fit into your garment easily. Don't forget to take your adjustment into account if there is any side-seam shaping.

GAUGE

Gauge controls both the shape and size of an article, so any variation, however slight, can distort the finished garment.

You must match the gauge given at the start of each pattern. To check your gauge, knit a square in the pattern stitch and/or stockinette stitch of perhaps 5–10 more stitches and 5–10 more rows than those given in the gauge note. Press the finished square under a damp cloth and mark out the central 4in/10cm square with pins. If you have too many stitches to 4in/10cm, try again using thicker needles. If you have too few stitches to 4in/10cm, try again using finer needles. Once you have achieved the correct gauge, your garment will be knitted to the measurements shown in the size diagram.

CABLE PATTERNS

Cable stitch patterns allow you to twist the stitches in various ways, to create decorative effects such as an interesting rope-like structure to the knitting. The cables can be thin and fine (just a couple of stitches wide) or big and chunky (up to 8 stitches or more).

To work cables, you need to hold the appropriate number of stitches that form the cable twist (abbreviated in pattern as C) on a separate small cable needle, while you knit behind or in front of them. You then knit the stitches off the cable needle before continuing to knit the remaining stitches in the row. Depending on whether the cable needle is at the front or the back of the work, the cables will twist to the left or right but the principle remains the same. A four-stitch cable will be abbreviated as C4F or C4B, depending on whether the cable needle is held to the front or back of the work.

COLORWORK

There are two main methods of working with color in knitted fabrics: the intarsia and the Fairisle techniques.

Intarsia

In the intarsia technique, you have to join in a new yarn color for each new block of color stitches. To prevent the yarns getting twisted on the ball, the simplest method is to make individual little balls of yarn, or bobbins, from pre-cut short lengths of yarn, one for each motif or block of color used in a row. You then work across the stitches, joining in the colors as required, by twisting them around each other where they meet on the wrong side of the work, to avoid gaps. You will need to neaten up the loose ends. They can either be darned along the color joins or they can be knitted in to the fabric as each color is worked by picking up the loops of the yarns carried across the back of the work as you knit.

Fairisle

When you are working a pattern with two or more repeating colors in the same row, you need to strand the yarn not in use behind the stitches being worked. This needs to be done with care, loosely enough to ensure that the strands not in use do not tighten and pucker the front of the knitting. To do this you need to treat the yarns not in use, known as "floating yarns," as if they were one yarn and spread the stitches as you work to their correct width to keep them elastic.

If you tend to knit colorwork too tightly, increase your needle size for the colorwork section.

FINISHING METHODS

Pressing

Block out each piece of knitting by pinning it on a board to the correct measurements in the pattern. Then lightly press it according to the ball band instructions, omitting any ribbed areas. Take special care to press the edges, as this makes sewing up easier and neater. If you cannot press the fabric, then cover the knitted fabric with a damp cloth and allow it to stand for a couple of hours. Darn in all ends neatly along the selvedge edge or a color join, as appropriate.

Stitching seams

When you stitch the pieces together, remember to match any areas of color and texture carefully where they meet. Use a special seam stitch, called mattress stitch, as it creates the neatest flattest seam. After all the seams are complete, press the seams and hems. Lastly, sew on the buttons to correspond with the positions of the buttonholes.

Making linings for bags

If you are knitting the bags in this book, it pays to line them carefully, using appropriate fabric. A good quality strong cotton is ideal for knitted bags as it provides some support for the fabric. Where the bag has a gusset at the base, you can add some extra strength to the base in the form of a cardboard liner, cut to the same size as the gusset. As you cannot wash the cardboard, you need to construct the liner so you can remove the cardboard easily.

It also pays to strengthen the straps of any bigger bags by wrapping the knitted pieces around a length of petersham ribbon, to make them less stretchy.

EMBROIDERY

For the patterns that use combinations of single daisy stitch (either as single stitches or to make a multi-petaled flower) and French knots (for the flower centers) the following shows how to work these.

Single daisy stitch

To make a single daisy stitch, bring your needle up then reinsert it in the same place, leaving a small loop. Bring the needle back out with the loop beneath the needle and make a small stitch over the loop to hold it in place. To make a flower shape, make a single daisy stitch and then create up to five more to form a little circle of stitches that resemble flower petals.

French knots

These are twists of thread made on top of each other to create a knot shape. Bring the needle through to the front of the fabric, wrap the thread around the needle tip a few times and, holding the yarn wraps with your fingertip, insert the needle back through the fabric where it came out and pull the thread through to the back.

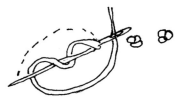

ABBREVIATIONS

alt	alternate
approx	approximately
beg	begin(s)(ning)
cm	centimeters
cont	continu(e)(ing)
dec	decreas(e)(ing)
DPN	double-pointed needle
foll	follow(s)(ing)
g	gram
in/"	inch(es)
inc	increase(e)(ing)
k	knit
k2tog	knit next 2 sts together
MC	main color
M1	make one st by picking up horizontal loop before next st and knitting into back of it
p	purl
patt	pattern
psso	pass slipped st over
p2sso	pass 2 sts over
p2tog	purl next 2 sts together
rem	remain(s)(ing)
rep	repeat
rev St st	reverse stockinette stitch
RS	right side
s2kp	slip 2 sts tog, k1, pass slipped sts over
skp	sl1, k1, psso
sk2p	sl1, k2tog, psso
sl 1	slip one st
sl2tog	slip 2 sts together
st(s)	stitch(es)
St st	stockinette stitch (1 row knit, 1 row purl)
tbl	through back of loop(s)
tog	together
WS	wrong side
yd	yard(s)
yo	yarn over needle
y2rn	yarn wrapped over needle twice
[ ]/*	repeat instructions within square brackets or between asterisks

YARN INFORMATION

The following are the specifications of the Rowan yarns used for the designs in this book. It is always best to try to obtain the exact yarns specified in the patterns, but when substituting yarns, remember to calculate the yarn amount needed by the yardage/meterage rather than by the ball weight. For yarn care directions, refer to the yarn label.

Pure Wool DK

Machine washable 100 percent pure wool; 1¾oz (approximately 137yd/125m) per ball. Recommended gauge: 22 sts and 30 rows to 4in/10cm in St st using size 6 (4mm) knitting needles.

Wool Cotton

A wool/cotton blend yarn; 50 percent merino wool, 50 percent cotton; 1¾oz (approximately 123yd/113m) per ball. Recommended gauge: 22–24sts and 30–32 rows to 4in/10cm in St st using size 5–6 (3.75–4mm) knitting needles.

Wool Cotton 4ply

A wool/cotton blend yarn; 50 percent merino wool, 50 percent cotton; 1¾oz (197yd/180m) per ball. Recommended gauge: 28sts and 36 rows to 4in/10cm in St st using size 2 (3.25mm) knitting needles.

Resources

U.S.A.
Westminster Fibers Inc,
8 Shelter Drive, Greer
South Carolina 29650
www.westminsterfibers.com

U.K.
Rowan, Green Lane Mill, Holmfirth,
West Yorkshire HD9 2DX
www.knitrowan.com

AUSTRALIA
Australian Country Spinners Pty Ltd,
Melbourne, Victoria 3004
tkohut@auspinners.com.au

AUSTRIA
Coats Harlander Ges GmbH
1210 Vienna
www.coatscrafts.at

BELGIUM
See Germany

BULGARIA
Coats Bulgaria
BG-1784 Sofia
www.coastsbulgaria.bg

CANADA
Westminster Fibers Inc,
Vaughan, Ontario L4H 3M8
www.westminsterfibers.coom

CHINA
Coats Shanghai Ltd, Shanghai
victor.li@coats.com

CYPRUS
See Bulgaria

DENMARK
Coats Expotex AB, Dalsjöfors
info.dk@coats.com

FINLAND
Coats Opti Crafts Oy, Kerava 04200
www.coatscrafts.fi

FRANCE
www.coatscrafts.fr

GERMANY
Coats GmbH, Kenzingen 79341
www.coatsgmbh.de

GREECE
See Bulgaria

HONG KONG
East Unity Company Ltd,
Chai Wan
eastunityco@yahoo.com.hk

ICELAND
Rowan At Storkurinn, Reykjavik 101
www.storkurinn.is

ITALY
Coats Cucirini srl, Milan 20126
www.coatscucirini.com

KOREA
Coats Korea Co. Lt,
Seoul 137-060
www.coatskorea.co.kr

LEBANON
y.knot, Saifi Village, Beirut
y.knot@cyberia.net.lb

LITHUANIA & RUSSIA
Coats Lietuva UAB,
Vilnius 09310
www.coatscrafts.lt

LUXEMBOURG
See Germany

NEW ZEALAND
ACS New Zealand, Christchurch
64 3 323 6665

NORWAY
Coats Knappehuset AS,
Bergen 5873
kundeservice@coats.com

PORTUGAL
Coats & Clark,
Vila Nova de Gaia 4400
351 223 770700

SINGAPORE
Golden Dragon Store, Singapore
058357
gdscraft@hotmail.com

SOUTH AFRICA
Arthur Bales Ltd, Johannesburg
2195
arthurb@new.co.za

SPAIN
Coats Fabra,
Barcelona 08030
www.coatscrafts.es

SWEDEN
Coats Expotex AB
kundtjanst@coats.com

SWITZERLAND
Coats Stroppel AG,
Untersiggenthal 5417
www.coatscrafts.ch

TAIWAN
Cactus Quality Co Ltd,
Taiwan, R.O.C. 10084
00886-2-23656527

THAILAND
Global Wide Trading,
Bangkok 10310
global.wide@yahoo.com

For all other countries please
contact Rowan for details

PUBLISHER'S ACKNOWLEDGMENTS

Thanks to everyone who contributed to the book, as mentioned by Martin in his acknowledgments right, and also to Light Locations and JJ Locations for the photography venues. And, indeed, to Martin himself for being such a delight to work with and so unfailingly professional at all times.

AUTHOR'S ACKNOWLEDGMENTS

A big thank you to the following team of people, without whose skills this book would not have been possible: Steven and Susan for their great work on photography, art direction, and styling, and to my niece Harriet for modeling so beautifully; Anne, for her elegant page layouts; our wonderful pattern writer, Penny, and her team of fantastic knitters; plus Katie and Marilyn, for their careful editing and checking; Frances for the beautifully knitted swatches; and the entire Rowan team for their continued support.

Finally, a special thank you, as ever, to my partner, Mark, Billy and Bunny (our adored cats!), and my loving family.